Table of Contents

This Page Intentionally Left Blank

Introduction

Background

This is the third in a series of Department of Defense Office of Inspector General (DoD OIG), Special Plans and Operations reports regarding establishment of an Office of Security Cooperation–Iraq (OSC-I). The first two assessments reported on planning and establishing the OSC-I, respectively, which occurred prior to the end of contingency operations and DoD transitioning the responsibility to train and equip the Iraq Security Forces (ISF) to Department of State (DOS). This third report deals with OSC-I mission capabilities and its post-contingency operating procedures including conducting security cooperation programs under the U.S. Mission in Iraq authority. This third assessment was conducted in coordination with DOS Office of Inspector General (DOS OIG), Office of Audits.

On August 25, 2011, the DoD IG issued Report No. SPO-2011-008, "Assessment of Planning for Transitioning the Security Assistance Mission in Iraq from Department of Defense to Department of State Authority." The report determined that, despite some shortcomings, detailed planning to accomplish the transition of the security assistance function to U.S. Mission authority was sufficiently developed and operative.

On March 16, 2012, the DoD Inspector General issued Report No. DODIG-2012-063, "Assessment of the DoD Establishment of the Office of Security Cooperation–Iraq." The report determined that, although the establishment of the OSC-I was on track to meet its full operating capability target date and to operate independently as an element of the U.S. Mission to Iraq by January, 2012, key areas required management attention.

DoD OIG and DOS OIG collaborated on a joint project to facilitate portions of this third DoD IG OSC-I report and to assist DOS OIG with its more comprehensive audit of the realignment of the U.S. diplomatic presence in Iraq. Two DOS OIG members accompanied the DoD OIG assessment team that visited Iraq in late 2012.

The objective of the joint DoD and DOS OIG project was to assess the process used to establish the short- and long-term staffing requirements for DoD elements assigned to the U.S. Mission in Iraq. It was conducted at U.S. Embassy–Baghdad, selected field locations in Iraq, and in Washington, D.C. The joint assessment included interviews in Washington, D.C., with DoD and DOS officials in bureaus and offices involved with staffing in Iraq, and interviews in Iraq with DoD and U.S. Mission program and management officials. DoD OIG and DOS OIG included relevant joint assessment aspects in their respective reports. There is no separate joint report.

Objectives

On August 16, 2012, DoD IG announced the "DoD IG Assessment of the Office of Security Cooperation–Iraq Mission Capability."

Specific objectives for this assessment were to:

- determine whether DoD goals, objectives, plans, and guidance for executing security cooperation programs in Iraq through the OSC-I performing under DOS/Chief of Mission authority are issued and sufficiently operative;
- determine whether the OSC-I is adequately structured and resourced to accomplish its security assistance/security cooperation mission;
- identify impediments to OSC-I mission accomplishment and provide suggested recommendations; and,
- assist the DOS OIG in assessing the process used to determine short-term and long-term OSC-I staffing requirements.

Strategic Partnership and U.S. Military Withdrawal

In February 2009 the President stated that, at the end of 2011, the U.S. would withdraw from Iraq in accordance with the existing Security Agreement that was signed with its government in 2008. However, the U.S. remained committed to an enduring strategic relationship between the two countries. This partnership was expressed and supported through the Strategic Framework Agreement, also signed in 2008, that stated the goal of a long term relationship between the U.S. and the Republic of Iraq was:

> …strengthening and development of democracy in Iraq, as well as ensuring that Iraq will assume full responsibility for its security, the safety of its people, and maintaining peace within Iraq and among the countries of the region.

The Security Agreement stipulated a complete U.S. military withdrawal from Iraq by the end of 2011. It also specified the status, principal provisions, and requirements that would regulate U.S. military forces during their temporary presence within Iraq through the period of their withdrawal at the end of December 2011. The President's plan was to reduce the U.S. military to a force of about 35,000 by August 2010 which would remain through the end of 2011 for the purpose of training, equipping, and advising the ISF. The U.S. Government sought a follow on bilateral security agreement[1] with Iraq that included necessary privileges and immunities for those DoD personnel who would not be assigned to the U.S. Embassy but who would operate in Iraq after the withdrawal of U.S. military forces. The inability of the two governments to reach such an agreement impeded post-2011 efforts to further defense cooperation relations.

Department of Defense Security Cooperation Overview

Security Cooperation – Security Assistance

Security cooperation consists of Department of Defense interactions with foreign defense establishments to build defense relationships that promote specific U.S. security interests, develop friendly military capabilities, and provide U.S. forces with peacetime and

---

[1] These type agreements are commonly referred to as Status of Forces Agreements, or SOFAs.

contingency access to a host nation. Security cooperation activities are implemented by DoD in coordination with the U.S. Chief of Mission in a partner nation (see Appendix D).

Security assistance administered by DoD is an important set of programs, but is only a portion of the many security cooperation programs involving DoD elements. The security assistance programs that DoD administers generally fall under DOS lead authority in an embassy, but are collectively considered a subset of security cooperation that is governed by provisions of United States Code (U.S.C.) 22 (see Appendix D).

The Defense Security Cooperation Agency (DSCA) is responsible for managing many DoD international programs through close coordination with security cooperation organizations (SCOs). SCOs, such as OSC-I, are important in-country points of contact that coordinate and assist in managing security cooperation activities between the U.S. and host nation governments, but geographic combatant commanders (GCCs), among other DoD elements, typically support and execute the major security cooperation activities within their respective theater of operation.

DoD Directive 5132.03, DoD Policy and Responsibilities Relating to Security Cooperation, indicates that security assistance and security cooperation activities were fundamental to achieving longer-term U.S. goals in Iraq. That policy states:

> Security cooperation, which includes DoD-administered security assistance programs, is an important tool of national security and foreign policy and is an integral element of the DoD mission. Security cooperation activities shall be planned, programmed, budgeted, and executed with the same high degree of attention and efficiency as other integral DoD activities. Security cooperation requirements shall be combined with other DoD requirements and implemented through standard DoD systems, facilities, and procedures.[2]

Broad Range of Security Cooperation Efforts

Besides security assistance, DoD has global responsibility for implementing a broad range of security cooperation programs (see Appendix D). To conduct those activities, it typically utilizes personnel from many DoD elements and numerous existing programmatic authorities. For example, in its area of operations, U.S. Central Command (USCENTCOM) has a major role implementing programs that are generally categorized as Combined Exercises and Military-to-Military Contacts.

Military-to-Military Contacts refers to programs that are designed to encourage a democratic orientation of defense establishments and military forces of other countries. One such program, the Combatant Commander Initiative Fund, was used in the case of Iraq to cover training, authority, and funding gaps for an interim period that occurred when Iraq Security Forces Fund (ISFF) authority expired in September 2012. Another program, Traditional Commander Activities (TCA), enables USCENTCOM to send small military liaison teams to partner countries for military to military training purposes.

---

[2] DoD Directive 5132.03, "DoD Policy and Responsibilities Relating to Security Cooperation," October 24, 2008.

It was unclear the extent to which and under what future security operating conditions USCENTCOM planned to use its TCA security cooperation authority in Iraq. The USCENTCOM Iraq Country Plan current at the time of this assessment did not address that level of detail.

Statutory Security Cooperation Arrangements

The Foreign Assistance Act (FAA) of 1961, as amended, states that the President may assign members of the U.S. Armed Forces to a foreign country to perform specific security assistance functions. Congress also stipulated that advisory and training assistance conducted by personnel assigned under the FAA shall be provided primarily by other personnel who are not assigned under the FAA and who are detailed for limited periods to perform specific tasks.[3]

Security cooperation organizations are located in foreign countries to coordinate and assist in managing security cooperation activities. In this regard, the OSC-I was unique because, besides those responsibilities and unlike security cooperation organizations in other countries, Congress also authorized it to conduct certain security cooperation tasks.

Security Sector Reform

Some of the security cooperation tasks that Congress authorized the OSC-I to conduct were activities that DoD routinely used to support DOS or U.S. Agency for International Development (USAID) Security Sector Reform (SSR) objectives. The SSR is a comprehensive, integrated U.S. Government approach to working with partner nations in such areas as defense and armed forces reform and national security planning and strategy support, among others. The U.S. Government recognizes the importance that well-developed partner nation security institutions have, particularly with respect to enhancing the effectiveness of U.S. security assistance efforts, and thereby, the building of long-term bilateral security relations.[4] A RAND Corporation study explains further how DoD leverages security cooperation efforts to support SSR.[5]

Contingency to Post-Contingency Transition in Iraq

Authorities and Funding

By December 2011, DoD had led U.S. efforts in Iraq with respect to security and military operations for nearly a decade. During that decade, Commander, USCENTCOM, with the policy guidance of the Chief of Mission (CoM), had been responsible for directing all U.S. Government (USG) efforts in support of organizing, equipping, and training the ISF.

---

[3] Foreign Assistance Act of 1961, as amended, §2321i, (a) and (b).

[4] Security Sector Reform, U.S. Agency for International Development, U.S. Department of State, U.S. Department of Defense, February 2009, pp. 1 – 3, www.state.gov/documents/organization/115810, accessed on January 30, 2013.

[5] What Works Best When Building Partner Capacity and Under What Circumstances?, RAND Monograph, Christopher Paul, et. al., pp. 8 – 10; http://www.rand.org/pubs/monographs/MG1253z1.html accessed on Feb 1, 2013.

To conduct contingency operations and support the development of ISF capability, Congress provided DoD with specific authority and funding that supported execution of operations, administration, and development of the ISF. For example, since 2005 the Iraq Security Forces Fund (ISFF) had provided for the U.S. military to equip and train the ISF. As Operation New Dawn (OND) ended in December 2011, DoD concluded contingency operations and transitioned lead responsibility for directing USG efforts that supported organizing, equipping, and training the ISF to DOS and CoM authority. This transition produced major changes, as well as associated challenges.

Major Department of Defense Post-contingency Support

Toward the close of 2010, DoD was asked to continue providing major support for U.S. Mission activities in Iraq. In January 2011, the Secretary of Defense approved a DOS request that DoD assume responsibility for security of DoD personnel in Iraq after December 31, 2011, as well as for managing several operating sites (hereinafter referred to as DoD managed field sites). CoM and USCENTCOM signed a memorandum of agreement (MOA) in January 2012 that further delineated the tasks each agency would accomplish regarding sustainment, support, and security at the DoD managed sites. Figure 1 depicts the geographical distribution of those sites and scope of DoD's investment of personnel utilized to accomplish major functions at each one.

Figure 1. DoD Managed Field Sites in Iraq

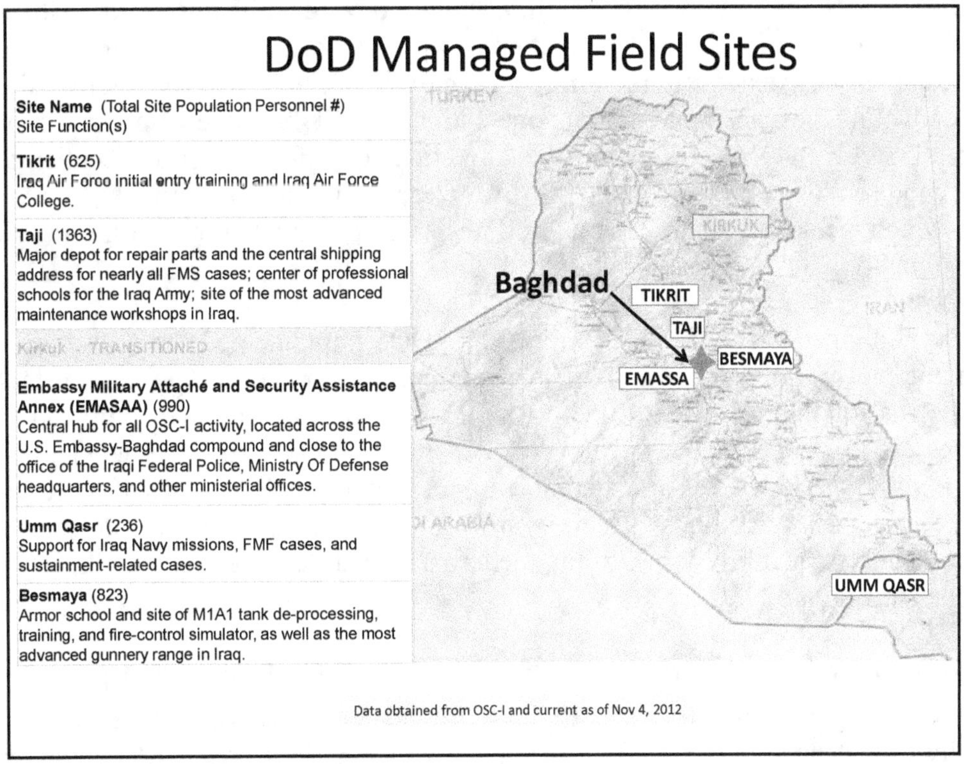

DoD Managed Field Sites

Site Name (Total Site Population Personnel #)
Site Function(s)

Tikrit (625)
Iraq Air Force initial entry training and Iraq Air Force College.

Taji (1363)
Major depot for repair parts and the central shipping address for nearly all FMS cases; center of professional schools for the Iraq Army; site of the most advanced maintenance workshops in Iraq.

Kirkuk - TRANSITIONED

Embassy Military Attaché and Security Assistance Annex (EMASAA) (990)
Central hub for all OSC-I activity, located across the U.S. Embassy-Baghdad compound and close to the office of the Iraqi Federal Police, Ministry Of Defense headquarters, and other ministerial offices.

Umm Qasr (236)
Support for Iraq Navy missions, FMF cases, and sustainment-related cases.

Besmaya (823)
Armor school and site of M1A1 tank de-processing, training, and fire-control simulator, as well as the most advanced gunnery range in Iraq.

Data obtained from OSC-I and current as of Nov 4, 2012

Source: OSC-I, November 4, 2012.

5

Special Congressional Authority

Congress granted the OSC-I authority to conduct training and advising activities in Iraq that other DoD elements, like USCENTCOM, would have normally performed in a country where the U.S. Government maintained a defense cooperation presence. The Department of Defense and Full-Year Continuing Appropriations Act, 2011 initially extended ISFF authority beyond the end of the contingency which allowed the U.S. military to continue providing assistance "including the provision of equipment, supplies, services, training, facility and infrastructure repair, and renovation" until that authority expired on September 30, 2012. At that point, USCENTCOM used an existing DoD program authority and funding—Combatant Commander Initiative Fund (CCIF)[6] —to sustain OSC-I training activities until the National Defense Authorization Act (NDAA) for Fiscal Year 2013 was enacted. That NDAA, signed in early January 2013, allowed the OSC-I to:

> …conduct non-operational training activities…in an institutional environment to address capability gaps, integrate processes relating to intelligence, air sovereignty, combined arms, logistics and maintenance, and to manage and integrate defense-related institutions.[7]

Organizational Structures and Lines of Communication

During Operation Iraqi Freedom (OIF), DoD utilized operational military organizational structures, procedures, and lines of communication to conduct its operations. This typically included deferring implementation of ISFF authorized activities to the joint operational military headquarters in Iraq. As an example, DoD tasked USCENTCOM with conducting the transition and implementation of the U.S. force withdrawal from Iraq, but USCENTCOM deferred most detailed transition planning and execution to U.S. Forces–Iraq (USF-I). By late 2010, USF-I was responsible for executing Operation New Dawn, which included withdrawing U.S. forces, transitioning responsibilities to DOS, and, ultimately, establishing OSC-I in 2011.

After the contingency ended in December 2011, DOS implemented activities through diplomatic means, procedures, and lines of communication in order to further establish the U.S. Mission Iraq. As DoD withdrew all troops and its operational command headquarters from Iraq, it continued to conduct significant activities that DOS would have ordinarily performed. For example, with respect to the Secretaries of State and Defense agreement regarding the security of DoD personnel in Iraq, DoD delegated considerable responsibility for fulfilling the terms of that agreement to USCENTCOM and, subsequently, to OSC-I.

Integration of the Office of Security Cooperation–Iraq

The OSC-I integration into the U.S. Embassy-Baghdad (USEMB-B) under CoM authority was planned to occur prior to contingency operations ending. USF-I Operations Order (OPORD) 11-01 stipulated that, by the time the OSC-I reached full operational

---

[6] U.S.C. 10 §166a, see Appendix C for more detailed information regarding CCIF.
[7] NDAA FY 2013, Section 1211, electronic page 351-352.

capability (FOC), no later than October 1, 2011, the OSC-I was to integrate into USEMB-B operations, processes, and procedures. Integration into the U.S. Mission is the normal posture for DoD security cooperation organizations.

To facilitate the transition from contingency operations, USCENTCOM provided latitude to USF-I to plan and execute the establishment of OSC-I. USF-I OPORD 11-01 included several tasks for establishing the OSC-I that incorporated shared oversight and responsibility of its activities between the U.S. Mission and USCENTCOM. For example, OPORD 11-01 tasked the USF-I Deputy Commanding General for Advising and Training (DCG A&T) with establishing the OSC-I. That OPORD also designated the DCG A&T to become Chief of the OSC-I and directed that USF-I transition its function of advising and training the ISF to the OSC-I by the time contingency operations ended.

DOS was expected to assume key lead responsibilities after contingency operations ended and OSC-I was to be a subordinate organization of the U.S. Mission. However, DOS did not receive funding to perform all required post-contingency responsibilities which resulted in DOS and CoM requesting assistance from DoD and USCENTCOM to provide security and logistics support at sites where OSC-I personnel resided and the OSC-I conducted its activities. The follow-on memorandum of agreement delineated the tasks each agency would accomplish to sustain, support, and secure its respective sites (see next section below and Appendix C, Memorandums of Agreement and Understanding). OSC-I became directly and uniquely involved in supporting significant DOS as well as DoD functions essential for implementing both security cooperation and security assistance activities.

Interagency Memorandum of Agreement

OSC-I being responsible for major additional duties produced a unique interagency division of labor in Iraq. In anticipation of the USF-I withdrawal, the U.S. Mission asked for and received additional enabler support from DoD for numerous activities that were not security cooperation or security assistance related. This included communications, explosive ordnance disposal, and intelligence expertise. To varying degrees, the OSC-I acted as the in-country DoD agent regarding support, management, and oversight of these activities. OSC-I was also responsible for operating the DoD managed field sites (which DoD also financed) that supported delivery of defense articles, services, and training through security assistance programs and where OSC-I and other DoD personnel resided. All of these factors led to the National Security Council (NSC) Deputies Committee approving an expanded OSC-I and DoD providing an increased number of personnel commensurate with its enhanced mission.

CoM and USCENTCOM entered into a formal memorandum of agreement in January 2012 to implement the terms of the Secretaries of State and Defense agreements.[8] Procedures at the OSC-I sites differed substantially from those managed by DOS, including security posture of the personnel at the sites and logistical support.

---

[8] See *Memorandums of Agreement and Understanding*, Appendix C, for additional information.

Privileges and Immunities

The security situation created by the uncertain environment [9] and lack of a status of forces agreement made DoD and USCENTCOM reluctant to deploy personnel to Iraq, other than those assigned to the embassy. This was because those personnel would not have specific diplomatic status or important privileges and immunities that a formal security agreement may have conferred. OSC-I personnel had a form of diplomatic status that differed from other DoD personnel in Iraq that operated under USCENTCOM authority. OSC-I personnel were assigned as administrative and technical staff of the U.S. Mission under CoM authority, [10] which provided them a formal status with privileges and immunities when on official duty. DoD therefore coordinated with DOS and the U.S. Mission to allow the OSC-I to conduct certain security cooperation and other related support activities. Congress granting OSC-I the authority to conduct those certain security cooperation and security assistance activities, which DoD, the DOS, and the U.S. Mission agreed were important at the time, enabled accomplishment of those activities in a manner that addressed DoD personnel security requirements.

Security Cooperation Strategy and Planning

Figure 2. Office of Security Cooperation–Iraq Strategy

Source: OSC-I

---

[9] Uncertain environment. JP 1-02, November 8, 2010, as amended through April 15, 2013. See Appendix C.

[10] U.S. Department of State, U.S. Department of State Foreign Affairs Manual Volume 2, July, 2013. http://www.state.gov/m/a/dir/regs/fam/02fam/0200/index.htm. See also Appendix C, *Privileges and Immunities* for additional information regarding this diplomatic status.

As of November 2012, the OSC-I had developed a mission statement and strategy framework that reflected national and U.S. Mission Iraq, as well as USCENTCOM Theater Campaign Plan and Iraq Country Plan objectives (see Figure 2). The lines of effort (that is, the large horizontal arrows in Figure 2 that indicated key focus areas) specifically included conducting security cooperation activities that supported ISF professionalization and leader development in support of strategic partnership goals and objectives. In general, these security cooperation activities supported Security Sector Reform, the previously mentioned U.S. Government initiative for furthering host nation security sector development efforts.[11]

Ongoing Transition of Responsibilities in Iraq

By November 2012, nearly a year after contingency operations ended, DOS-directed personnel reductions at U.S. Embassy Iraq required accelerating control of DoD managed field site facilities back to the Iraqi government, completing the transition of responsibilities for providing various types of logistical and specialized DoD support from DoD to DOS, and integrating the OSC-I into the U.S. Mission.

The depiction in Figure 3 summarizes how authorities, funding, organizational structures, and lines of communication changed when contingency operations ended in Iraq at the end of 2011 and the post-contingency operating environment began, albeit not yet a normal, steady state peacetime situation. It also projects how these factors may eventually evolve and emphasizes important conditions that existed when the DoD OIG team visited Iraq in late 2012.

Figure 3. Transition of DoD and DOS Responsibilities in Iraq

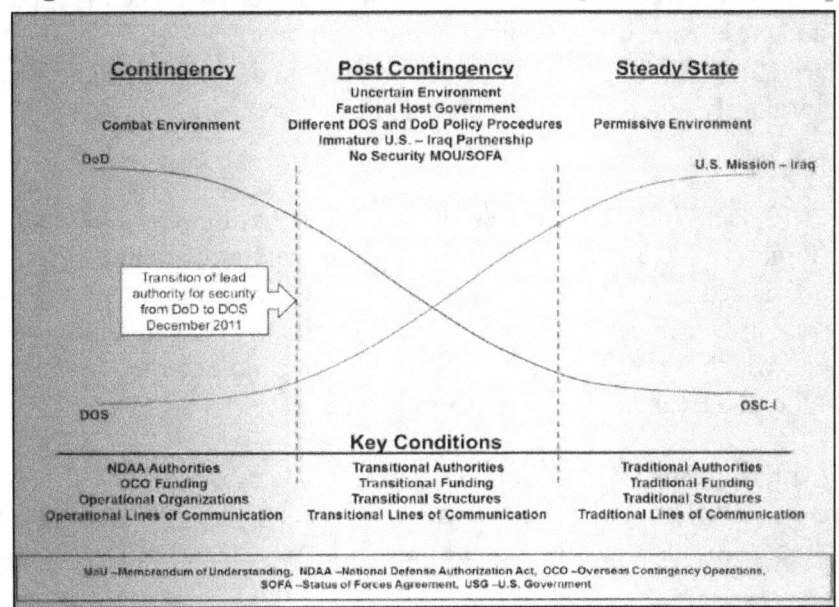

Source: DoD OIG SPO.

---

[11] See *Size of the OSC-I*, Appendix C, for additional background information.

Key conditions that applied during the DoD OIG assessment included:

- uncertain, less than fully permissive security environment;
- factional host nation government;
- different DOS and DoD support and security cooperation implementation arrangements and procedures than found in other countries where a SCO resides;
- immature U.S.-Iraq partnership and inter-governmental relationships; and,
- no status of forces agreement.

State Department Staffing Reductions

According to DOS OIG reporting, DOS used a multi-phased, percentage-based approach to reduce U.S. Mission staff personnel in Iraq from 16,298 to a planned 6,320 by January 2014. Instead of fully considering U.S. foreign policy priorities, DOS and Embassy Baghdad applied three primary approaches to achieve an overall 61 percent staffing reduction—across-the-board reductions for direct hire staff and some security contractors, reductions in the amount of life support services provided, and the closure of sites throughout Iraq outside of the main embassy compound in Baghdad. Specifically, DOS directed that the following series of staff reductions be achieved by the indicated dates:

- October 2012: a 17 percent across-the-board reduction of direct hire staff, a 25 percent reduction in security staff, and the closure of the Baghdad Police Academy Annex and the Mission facilities in Kirkuk.
- October 2013: a cumulative 25 percent across-the-board reduction of direct hire and contractor staff, the closure of most of the Embassy Annex Prosperity work site, and the closure of the Erbil Diplomatic Support Center.
- January 2014: a cumulative 61 percent reduction of direct hire and contractor staff, primarily as a result of additional site closures, for a final total of 6,320 staff.[12]

By October 2012, DOS included the OSC-I in its U.S. Mission personnel reduction efforts. The largest reduction of overall OSC-I personnel involved transitioning all DoD managed and financed field sites back to the government of Iraq. Site transitions were to occur by the end of December 2013 and included physically consolidating the core OSC-I element, which was at Embassy Military Attaché and Security Assistance Annex (EMASAA), into the Baghdad Embassy Complex (BEC).

Discussions with DoD and DOS personnel regarding the impact of OSC-I personnel reductions revealed differing views concerning the role and scope of the OSC-I mission and its objectives. For instance, the Department of Defense and Full-Year Continuing

---

[12] "Audit of the U.S. Mission Iraq Staffing Process," United States Department of State and the Broadcasting Board of Governors Office of the Inspector General, AUD-MERO-13-33, August 2013, pg. 7.

Appropriations Act, 2011 initially extended the ISFF authority that enabled OSC-I to conduct security cooperation and authorized funding for those activities through September 30, 2012. By that time the OSC-I had expanded to about 260 core billets. The NDAA for FY 2013 eventually extended some of the OSC-I ISF training provisions and funded the expanded OSC-I through September 30, 2013.

Regardless, some in DOS and DoD viewed the OSC-I size as too large in relation to other security cooperation organizations, overreaching in the number of security cooperation and support activities it was performing, and wanted to reduce its personnel numbers. However, military leaders charged with implementing security cooperation in Iraq perceived a continuing need for the OSC-I to conduct priority security cooperation activities that other DoD elements were precluded from performing because of a lack of a status of forces agreement. In addition, the DoD-DOS arrangement allowed for the OSC-I performing certain mission support activities. The combination of increased mission and support responsibilities required more personnel than would be authorized under the personnel reduction plan. Lack of common definitions and terminology with respect to the role of security cooperation and the various DOS and DoD transition activities tended to perpetuate these two differing viewpoints.

There was no commonly shared view of what a normal U.S. Mission presence consisted of in Iraq. OSC-I goals included ultimately achieving a "normalized configuration" (see Figure 2 on page 8, the last Desired Operational State in the bottom right corner), and the immediate DOS-directed personnel reductions were aimed at achieving a "more normalized embassy presence." However, there was no specific agreed-upon definition for what a normalized U.S. Mission presence or configuration is or whether the personnel reduction plan scheduled for OSC-I was consistent with implementing U.S. defense cooperation and strategic partnering objectives with respect to Iraq. In an October 2012 interview with the DOS OIG, the U.S. Ambassador to Iraq stated that normalization was "less of a defined term than a mental concept of acknowledging that we are not normal now [and that a normal presence is when an embassy is] not breaking all the rules [and that Iraq has moved] from being an exceptional to a more standard embassy."

Moreover, there was no evidence of a clear consensus between DOS and DoD/OSC-I regarding the security cooperation mission of the OSC-I, or the number of OSC-I personnel necessary and drawdown timetable necessary to ensure it was accomplished. One focus of this disagreement concerned the rate at which certain OSC-I mission and support capabilities should be reduced to assume a more normalized state. To some in DOS and DoD, achieving U.S. Mission staffing goals involved reducing the number of OSC-I personnel to meet DOS personnel targets, while organizationally realigning its functions to more closely resemble that of other SCOs. Military leaders tasked with implementing security cooperation and building a bilateral partnership with Iraq in an uncertain security environment favored a more deliberate planning process to determine personnel reductions. To them, personnel reductions needed to be based on U.S. policy priorities, resource requirements, and progress in developing defense cooperation that fully considered the OSC-I's ability to support USCENTCOM theater and Iraq-specific planning objectives. OSC-I planners consequently wanted to ensure that the transition of

DoD managed sites back to the government of Iraq occurred in a manner that enabled effective follow-on, contractor-based security assistance activities at those locations as they expected would be required.

Some DoD and DOS personnel considered 59 a notional baseline number of personnel for what should comprise the OSC-I in order to accomplish its mission. However, an OSC-I configured in that baseline manner would no longer be able to conduct security cooperation in accordance with how its mission was then currently understood and defined by OSC-I analysis. That baseline configuration would consist of 46 permanent personnel to assist in coordinating and managing security assistance and 13 to assist in coordinating and managing other security cooperation efforts.

Observation 1. Scope of the Office of Security Cooperation–Iraq Mission

The OSC-I lacked clearly defined responsibilities with respect to its security cooperation mission in Iraq.

This occurred because the OSC-I, which functioned differently than other security cooperation organizations, was not informed by theater and Iraq-specific country level security cooperation plans that had been updated to reflect current DoD priorities and operating realities. Further, updated planning details had not been coordinated with and agreed to by the U.S. Mission, DOS, and DoD.

Additionally, DoD had not designated a Senior Defense Official/Defense Attaché (SDO/DATT) at the U.S. Mission Iraq and had not otherwise clearly specified the roles and responsibilities of the senior DoD official assigned to Iraq.

Lack of clearly defined responsibilities inhibited focused efforts by the OSC-I and unity of effort between the OSC-I and the U.S. Mission. A clearly focused and scoped security cooperation role, informed by current geographic military theater and Iraq-specific security priorities like those that updated plans would have provided, was needed. Without that basis, the OSC-I and U.S. Mission were at risk of not accomplishing security cooperation program activities important to the development of bilateral security relations with Iraq.

Applicable Criteria

DoD Directive 5132.03, "DoD Policy and Responsibilities Relating to Security Cooperation," October 24, 2008.

Defense Security Cooperation Agency Manual 5105.38-M, "Security Assistance Management Manual," updated through April 2013 (http://www.dsca.osd.mil/samm/).

Joint Publication 5-0, "Joint Operation Planning," August 11, 2011.

Foreign Affairs Act of 1961, as amended, "Legislation on Foreign Relations Through 2008," Section 515, March 2010.

Discussion

The Conduct of Security Cooperation in Iraq

Security cooperation organizations normally function as part of the diplomatic staff at the various U.S. embassies under CoM authority and primarily serve as in-country points of contact between the U.S. Government and the host nation. While those organizations

> *Security cooperation organizations do not normally conduct security cooperation*

assist in coordinating and supporting security cooperation efforts, other DoD elements[13] typically manage the various security cooperation programs and conduct implementation activities. Arrangements between DOS and DoD for conducting security cooperation in Iraq were unlike those in other countries.[14]

The OSC-I was responsible for conducting security cooperation activities in Iraq that other DoD elements, including the Combatant Command, would have normally performed in a country where the U.S. Government maintained a defense cooperation presence. Without a status of forces agreement, DoD was hesitant to deploy personnel to Iraq because they would lack privileges and immunities that DoD required. As administrative and technical staff of the U.S. Mission under Chief of Mission authority, OSC-I personnel had a form of diplomatic status that other DoD personnel who operated under USCENTCOM authority in Iraq did not possess.[15] This included a form of formal diplomatic privileges and immunities when on official duty. To mitigate DoD security concerns, DOS agreed to allow the OSC-I to conduct some security cooperation activities that DoD considered essential to supporting priority regional and Iraq-specific military security objectives.

> *The OSC-I was responsible for conducting security cooperation activities in Iraq that other DoD elements would have normally performed*

OSC-I officials often cited the ministerial training that its Senior Advisors' Group[16] conducted, as well as efforts to enhance Iraqi professional military education as examples of such priority DoD security cooperation efforts. In general, those efforts supported SSR, a U.S. Government initiative that sought to improve a partner nation's security and enhance security assistance effectiveness by developing its leaders and institutions. SSR implementation guidance for DOS and DoD practitioners stressed the importance of a comprehensive, fully integrated foreign assistance approach, to include DoD security cooperation activities.[17,18]

DoD leveraged the OSC-I in other unique ways. The CoM is usually responsible for U.S. Mission staff, but the Secretaries of State and Defense agreed DoD would assume responsibility for the security of its personnel in Iraq, as well as for supporting and

---

[13] Examples of those elements include combatant command, like USCENTCOM, military departments, and OSD agencies. "The Management of Security Cooperation," (Green Book) 32nd Edition, January 2013, Defense Institute of Security Assistance Management, pg. 1-1.

[14] See the Introduction for additional information regarding security cooperation arrangements in Iraq.

[15] See Privileges and Immunities, Appendix C.

[16] See Senior Advisors' Group, Appendix C.

[17] "Security Sector Reform," U.S. Agency for International Development, U.S. Department of State, U.S. Department of Defense, February 2009, pp. 1,3,&6, www.state.gov/documents/organization/115810.pdf, accessed on January 30, 2013.

[18] "What Works Best When Building Partner Capacity and Under What Circumstances?," RAND Monograph, Christopher Paul, et. al., pp. 8 – 10; http://www.rand.org/pubs/monographs/MG1253z1.html accessed on Feb 1, 2013.

managing various field operating sites. CoM and Commander, USCENTCOM signed a MOA in January 2012 establishing separate responsibilities at diplomatic DOS properties and DoD managed sites in Iraq.[19] The OSC-I, though still part of the diplomatic staff, assumed many of those responsibilities, making it directly responsible to DoD for the conduct of major security cooperation and other support activities. This arrangement, which altered customary lines of authority and interactions between the U.S. Mission and the OSC-I, caused the OSC-I to function somewhat autonomously with respect to the conduct of these DoD functions (see Observation 3).

OSC-I officials were concerned that reducing or eliminating their ability to conduct certain priority security cooperation activities would jeopardize attaining desired security objectives in Iraq, at least as long as other DoD elements were precluded from performing those activities. Some other DOS and DoD officials did not share that concern, but, in certain instances, those officials also did not fully appreciate the security cooperation activities that DoD had planned for Iraq post-2011. For example, senior U.S. Mission officials that questioned the utility of OSC-I's Senior Advisors' Group activities were unaware that the USCENTCOM Iraq Country Plan, a major source of DoD security cooperation objectives, priorities, and other details for Iraq, included those type activities as key tasks.

Planning and Coordination

The lack of updated USCENTCOM Theater Campaign and Iraq Country Plans was a main factor impeding overall unity of effort with respect to the OSC-I mission and resources required for accomplishing it. As of January 2013, those plans were dated

> *Operating arrangements and conditions in Iraq had changed considerably since USCENTCOM had issued its latest Theater Campaign and Iraq Country Plans*

January 2012 and October 2011, respectively. However, after contingency operations ended in December 2011 and DoD transitioned its lead authority for development of ISF capability to DOS, command and support relationships between DOS and DoD, to include authorities and the operational environment and conditions in Iraq, changed considerably. It was thus unclear whether those plans reflected current DoD priorities or operating realities. For example, as of February 2013, evidence provided to the DoD IG showed that the OSC-I mission, strategy, and security cooperation activities and the Iraq Country Plan reflected senior leader professional development and focusing on improving ISF intelligence fusion and dissemination as essential tasks for meeting Theater Campaign Plan intermediate military objectives. At that time, USCENTCOM officials indicated they had no plans to deploy personnel to perform those tasks if the OSC-I personnel capability to do so was eliminated. USCENTCOM officials stated that Iraq would either have to pay to have the activities performed, as normal security assistance programs required, or else they would not be accomplished. As a

---

[19] See *Memorandums of Agreement and Understanding*, Appendix C.

15

consequence, OSC-I officials were uncertain whether higher DoD echelons shared the same objectives and priorities they had identified at their level.

Updated USCENTCOM Theater Campaign and Iraq Country Plans are necessary to frame, clarify, and verify current strategic and operational guidance and theater objectives for implementation at OSC-I levels. Besides revised objectives, assumptions, and operating conditions, updated planning details needed to include additional specifics related to contingency options[20] that addressed important variations in conditions and assumptions that were most likely to impact achieving desired outcomes. Details also needed to provide updated criteria, with measures of effectiveness and measures of performance for assessing progress towards meeting the desired states. In January 2013, one senior USCENTCOM official stated the Iraq Country Plan needed updating but did not specify when that would occur. That official also noted that USCENTCOM was to get a new commander, which could delay the revision of those plans.

Coordinating updated USCENTCOM planning details with the U.S. Mission, DOS, and DoD would have facilitated effective communication and mutual understanding of the OSC-I mission. Senior OSC-I leaders have initiated dialogue with higher DoD echelons and with the U.S. Mission to clarify strategic guidance, responsibilities, and priorities, but with limited success. In addition to the lack of current USCENTCOM plans, agencies and sections at the U.S. Mission had not received DOS guidance regarding functions, factors, or skills to consider when eliminating personnel or positions. This included OSC-I personnel and positions (see Observation 2). In addition, neither DOS nor the U.S. Mission had developed a specific, agreed-upon definition for what constituted a normalized diplomatic presence, particularly as it would apply to OSC-I.

> *Coordinating updated USCENTCOM planning details with and seeking agreement between the U.S. Mission, DOS, and DoD would have helped facilitate effective communication*

Designating a Senior Defense Department Official in Iraq

DoD did not designate a SDO/DATT at the U.S. Mission in Iraq, which further contributed to a lack of clearly defined OSC-I responsibilities. DoD Directive 5105.75, "Department of Defense Operations at U.S. Embassies," stipulates that:

> Unified DoD representation in U.S. embassies is critical to the accomplishment of national security objectives....[and that]...The SDO/DATT is the CoM's principal military advisor on defense and national security issues, the senior diplomatically accredited DoD military officer assigned to a U.S. diplomatic mission, and the single

---

[20] This is commonly referred to as branch, or sequel, planning. JP 1-02, "Department of Defense Dictionary of Military and Associated Terms," November 8, 2010 (as amended through December 15, 2013), pp. 33 and 264.

point of contact for all DoD matters involving the embassy or DoD elements assigned to or working from the embassy.[21]

That directive enumerates specific responsibilities of the SDO/DATT,[22] and further identifies the Under Secretary of Defense for Policy as the official that appoints selected officers to that position, on behalf of the Secretary of Defense.

In February 2012, USCENTCOM formally requested the Director for Strategic Plans and Policy, Joint Staff, support concurrently designating the Chief of the OSC-I as SDO in Iraq. Justification for Secretary of Defense making that determination included creating a single point of contact for both DoD and CoM to facilitate intra- and inter-departmental communication, as stipulated by DoD Directive 5105.75. Despite numerous staff exchanges regarding this request over ensuing months, as of April 2013, DoD had not appointed neither an SDO/DATT nor an SDO in Iraq.

Conclusion

While authorized to *conduct* security cooperation and an expanded range of support activities, DOS and DoD officials disagreed about the scope of OSC-I activities. In relation to other security cooperation organizations, some in DOS and DoD viewed the OSC-I as too large and overreaching in the number of mission and support activities it performed. Military leaders charged with executing security cooperation in Iraq valued the OSC-I for conducting priority activities that other DoD elements were precluded from performing.

Failure to establish consensus regarding the scope of the OSC-I mission and support responsibilities that reflected the full range of planned DoD security cooperation priorities inhibited accomplishing efforts important to developing the Iraqi government's security sector and furthering bilateral security relations with Iraq. Disagreement between DOS and DoD officials detracted from overall unity of effort and resulted in mixed signals, confused mission objectives, and unclear lines of authority, particularly in Baghdad between the U.S. Mission and the OSC-I. Updated theater and Iraq-specific country level plans were necessary to verify current priorities, otherwise reducing or eliminating OSC-I capabilities increased the risk that important DoD security cooperation efforts in Iraq would not be accomplished. Further, incomplete planning and coordination exacerbated inter- and intra-agency communications, especially since there was no specific, agreed-upon definition for what constituted a normalized U.S. Mission presence.

Until other DoD elements can perform their usual activities, restricting OSC-I ability to perform key activities would compromise accomplishment of U.S. strategic military objectives. It would inhibit developing the ISF, especially development of Iraqi senior

---

[21] DoD Directive 5105.75, "Department of Defense Operations at U.S. Embassies," December 21, 2007, pg. 2.
[22] See Appendix D for a listing of SDO/DATT responsibilities. Ibid, pp. 7-8.

leaders and Iraqi institutions, which were fundamental to DoD supporting critical U.S. national level interests.

Recommendations, Management Comments, and Our Response

Recommendation

> 1.a. Under Secretary of Defense for Policy, in coordination with Department of State counterparts and Commander, U.S. Central Command:
>
> 1.a.(1) clearly specify the nature and scope of Office of Security Cooperation–Iraq mission activities, to include security assistance, as well as necessary security cooperation activities;

Management Comments

Under Secretary of Defense for Policy. In responding for the Under Secretary of Defense for Policy, the Principal Director for Middle East Policy agreed but did not further specify the action they had taken or planned to take to implement the recommendation.

Our Response

Under Secretary of Defense for Policy comments were partially responsive. Although agreeing, comments did not specify the action they had taken or planned to take to implement the recommendation. We therefore request that the Under Secretary of Defense for Policy provide additional comments to the final report that clearly specify the nature and scope of Office of Security Cooperation–Iraq mission activities, to include security assistance and other security cooperation activities necessary for achieving U.S. Central Command Theater Campaign Plan and Iraq Country Plan objectives within the uncertain environment that exists in Iraq.

Recommendation

> 1.a. Under Secretary of Defense for Policy, in coordination with Department of State counterparts and Commander, U.S. Central Command:
>
> 1.a.(2) take action to ensure interagency information exchange at all DoD echelons is sufficient to effectively plan and execute approved security cooperation activities in Iraq, to include defining a normal Office of Security Cooperation–Iraq organizational construct with specific functions; and,

Management Comments

Under Secretary of Defense for Policy. In responding for the Under Secretary of Defense for Policy, the Principal Director for Middle East Policy agreed but did not further specify the action they had taken or planned to take to implement the recommendation.

Our Response

Under Secretary of Defense for Policy comments were partially responsive. Although agreeing, comments did not specify the action they had taken or planned to take to implement the recommendation. We therefore request that the Under Secretary of Defense for Policy provide additional comments to the final report that specify the action they have taken or plan to take to ensure interagency information exchange at all DoD echelons is sufficient to effectively plan and execute approved security cooperation activities in Iraq. Response should sufficiently detail the specific functions that need to be performed, as well as define an Office of Security Cooperation–Iraq organizational construct that is appropriate for performing those functions within the uncertain environment that exists in Iraq.

Recommendation

> 1.a. Under Secretary of Defense for Policy, in coordination with Department of State counterparts and Commander, U.S. Central Command:
>
> 1.a.(3) designate a Senior Defense Official with clearly specified and fully coordinated responsibilities in Iraq.

Management Comments

Under Secretary of Defense for Policy. In responding for the Under Secretary of Defense for Policy, the Principal Director for Middle East Policy agreed but did not further specify the action they had taken or planned to take to implement the recommendation.

Unsolicited Comments

Although not required to comment, Joint Staff provided the following comments. For the full text of the Joint Staff comments, see Appendix F.

Joint Staff. In a consolidated Joint Staff response, the Deputy Director, Joint Education and Doctrine, Joint Staff J-7, stated that Joint Staff J-5 agreed and that the Chief of the Office of Security Cooperation–Iraq will perform Senior Defense Official duties until the security cooperation office transitions to a traditional security office.

Our Response

Under Secretary of Defense for Policy comments were partially responsive. Although agreeing, comments did not specify the action they had taken or planned to take to implement the recommendation. We therefore request that the Under Secretary of Defense for Policy provide additional comments to the final report that specify the action they have taken or plan to take to officially designate a Senior Defense Official with clearly specified and fully coordinated responsibilities in Iraq.

Recommendation

1.b. Commander, U. S. Central Command issue an updated Theater Campaign Plan and, in coordination with U.S. Chief of Mission in Iraq, an updated Iraq Country Plan.

Management Comments

U.S. Central Command. Responding for the Commander, the U.S. Central Command Inspector General Executive Director agreed and further stated that U.S. Central Command issued an updated Theater Campaign Plan on March 15, 2013, with revised security cooperation details for Iraq, as well as an updated Iraq Country Security Cooperation Plan that was developed in coordination with Office of Security Cooperation–Iraq and synchronized with the FY 2014 Department of State Mission Resource Request for Iraq.

Joint Staff. Although not required to comment, a consolidated Joint Staff response from the Deputy Director, Joint Education and Doctrine, Joint Staff J-7, stated that Joint Staff J-5 agreed and that J-5 continued to coordinate with U.S. Central Command as that command updates its theater and Iraq-specific plans.

Our Response

U.S. Central Command comments were partially responsive. We commend U.S. Central Command for issuing updated plans with revised security cooperation details for Iraq. We request that the command forward copies of those plans in response to the final report for our review. Further, we request U.S. Central Command provide specific information regarding the extent to which the U.S. Chief of Mission in Iraq agreed with the objectives of the updated Iraq Country Security Cooperation Plan, resources required, and level of risk that will be accepted to support accomplishing tasks and activities to achieve its objectives.

Observation 2. Sizing the Office of Security Cooperation–Iraq

The ongoing process used by DOS to direct OSC-I personnel reductions has not fully considered important DoD security cooperation mission objectives and priorities with respect to Iraq.

This occurred because the DOS implemented its process for determining U.S. Mission Iraq personnel reductions, which did not follow established DOS organizational "rightsizing" methodology, as a primarily top-down directed initiative in which cuts were made based on percentages and targets across assigned agencies without sufficient consideration of their differing missions and resource requirements.

Moreover, reductions in OSC-I staffing were made without having first conducted a joint DOS, CoM, DoD, and USCENTCOM coordinated analysis of U.S. defense relations-building objectives with respect to Iraq and OSC-I's defense cooperation role and responsibilities in support of this mission.

As a result, OSC-I's capacity to accomplish its mission could be impeded and therefore its contribution to achieving U.S. bilateral policy objectives diminished.

Applicable Criteria

GAO-03-396, "Overseas Presence: Rightsizing Framework Can be Applied at U.S. Diplomatic Posts in Developing Countries," (Washington, D.C.: April, 2003).

Discussion

DOS OIG determined that the DOS process for determining U.S. Mission Iraq staffing requirements did not fully consider U.S. foreign policy priorities specific to Iraq. Instead, DOS and Embassy Baghdad primarily applied other approaches to reduce its staff numbers that included across-the-board reductions for direct hire staff and some security contractors, reductions in the amount of life support provided, and the closure of sites throughout Iraq.[23] Consequently, even though the U.S. Mission Iraq and the OSC-I did negotiate a reduced number of OSC-I personnel and developed a plan for achieving those numbers by the end of fiscal year 2013, including the OSC-I in overall DOS staffing reduction efforts could cause its staffing numbers and skill composition to be misaligned with mission requirements and priorities.

The Rightsizing Framework and Methodology

DOS OIG reporting stated the GAO established a framework and methodology for rightsizing embassies that aligns the number of staff with foreign policy priorities at

---

[23] "Audit of the U.S. Mission Iraq Staffing Process," United States Department of State and the Broadcasting Board of Governors Office of the Inspector General, AUD-MERO-13-33, August 2013, pg. 7.

overseas diplomatic posts.[24] GAO defined rightsizing as aligning the number and location of staff assigned overseas with foreign policy priorities and security and other constraints.[25] One framework consideration that especially applied to OSC-I was: Are any mission priorities not being addressed?[26]

Oversight organizations had emphasized the importance of establishing mission priorities for the purposes of determining overseas mission staffing. In a 2005 inspection, DOS OIG cited the complexities of rightsizing in high-threat posts and reinforced the importance of posts identifying mission priorities to serve as a baseline for determining staff levels.[27] A more recent Secretary of State directed review on Benghazi, Libya, also recommended that posts in high threat areas have a "defined, attainable, and prioritized mission."[28]

Establishment of Broader U.S. Mission Priorities

DOS OIG determined that the U.S. diplomatic mission did not fully consider U.S. foreign policy priorities or provide guidance to support its staff reductions. As reported by DOS OIG, DOS may have established policy priorities for Iraq, but neither DOS nor embassy officials in Iraq could show how staffing levels, whether for overall staffing or for specific agencies and sections, were systematically assessed using those priorities as criteria to support the reductions. Nor had the U.S. Embassy communicated sufficient guidance to agencies or its section leaders on the factors to consider when selecting positions to eliminate. Sections and agency leaders consequently had to apply their own criteria for determining which positions to retain and which to eliminate. Most sections and agencies, to include the OSC-I, initially eliminated unfilled positions, followed by those that had recently, or soon would, become vacant.[29]

> *The U.S. diplomatic mission did not establish priorities or provide guidance to support its staff reductions*

According to DOS OIG reporting, DOS officials indicated that other considerations took precedence over establishing mission priorities in the decisions to reduce U.S. Mission Iraq staffing. DOS OIG reporting stated DOS officials indicated that congressional and White House concerns over high costs and security vulnerabilities associated with operating in Iraq were primary considerations for the staffing reductions instead of a

---

[24] Ibid, pp. 7-8.

[25] GAO-03-396,"Overseas Presence Rightsizing Framework Can Be Applied at U.S. Diplomatic Posts in Developing Countries," (Washington, D.C.: April, 2003).

[26] GAO-02-659T, "Overseas Presence: Observations on a Rightsizing Framework," (Washington, D.C.: May, 2002).

[27] Department of State Office of Inspector General, "Rightsizing the U.S. Government Presence Overseas: A Progress Report," ISP-I-06-11, December 2005.

[28] Mullen, et. al, "Accountability Review Board, Report on the Events of September 11, 2012, at the U.S. Consulate General Benghazi, Libya (Unclassified)," U.S. Department of State, (Washington, D.C.: Dec. 18, 2012), http://www.state.gov/documents/organization/202446.pdf accessed on Feb. 15, 2013.

[29] Ibid, pp. 7, 9, and 14.

systematic analysis.[30] In regard to security vulnerabilities, the DOS OIG specifically cited the DOS December 2012 Accountability Review Board report on the September 2012 attacks on various compounds in Benghazi, Libya, as reinforcing the need for, and importance of, "defined, attainable, and prioritized mission[s]" to justify the risks and operating costs. As reported to the DOS OIG, DOS officials indicated that these and other factors influenced DOS in when and how they imposed staff cuts and precluded completing an analysis that linked staffing requirements to priorities.[31]

Potential for Position and Skill Gaps

DOS OIG determined that, without a systematic staffing analysis based on U.S. foreign policy priorities specific to Iraq, DOS could not support that its planned staff size would provide the proper number or skill mix of personnel needed to meet U.S. Mission priorities while minimizing security risk and optimizing costs. In addition, across-the-board reductions did not discriminate between specific functions, personnel skills, and programs nor consider how agencies' activities contributed to overarching U.S. policy goals. Delegating staff reduction decisions without guidance on functional or programmatic priorities also raised potential questions regarding the alignment of mission priorities and staff skill requirements.[32] OSC-I officials indicated that it may have eliminated positions and skills that were required for current and future security cooperation activities and retained other positions and skills that were no longer needed.

OSC-I Mission Analysis

As of November 2012, the OSC-I was operating from a mission statement and strategy framework that linked desired end states with the stated national and DoD theater level objectives through four lines of operation (that is, areas of focused effort).[33] Each line of operation broadly specified the security assistance and cooperation activities OSC-I employed to promote related objectives (see Figure 2, Introduction). OSC-I officials expressed a common understanding of the mission, activities, and objectives that had been defined at their level. Notably, OSC-I's mission set included conducting security cooperation activities – a special case, unlike that found at other security cooperation organizations (see Observation 1).

Though OSC-I determined its required activities through a deliberate mission analysis process, that analysis was not based on updated USCENTCOM security cooperation planning details. By February 2013, the USCENTCOM Theater Campaign Plan and Iraq Country Plan were dated January 2012 and October 2011, respectively. By that time, as part of its efforts to support the DOS-directed personnel reductions, the OSC-I had completed its mission risk analysis for performing the activities necessary to achieve

---

[30] Congressional concerns included development and assistance programs. See S-PRT 112-34, "Iraq Report: Political Fragmentation And Corruption Stymie Economic Growth And Political Progress," Minority Staff Trip Report to the Committee on Foreign Relations, U.S. Senate, 112th Congress, (Washington, D.C.: April 30, 2012).

[31] Ibid, pp. 8, 12 – 13.

[32] Ibid, pp. 1, 9, and 15.

[33] OSC-I lines of operation. See Appendix C and Figure 2, Introduction.

Iraq-specific security cooperation objectives. But, that analysis was based on the aforementioned USCENTCOM plans, versus updated planning details that had been fully coordinated between DOS, CoM, DoD, USCENTCOM, and the OSC-I (see Observation 1).

OSC-I Personnel Reductions

DOS initially directed OSC-I reduce its staff of about 260 personnel by 60 billets around the same time its authority to conduct advisory and training assistance expired on October 1, 2012. At that time, DoD was coordinating with Congress to extend that authority. OSC-I officials stated that, before language was incorporated into the NDAA for FY 2013 and it was passed, USCENTCOM ordered the OSC-I to eliminate security cooperation mission billets that included the term "assist" in their position descriptions. The OSC-I identified and eliminated 27 billets that met that criterion. Shortly thereafter, USCENTCOM also reportedly directed that the OSC-I eliminate another 20 billets from its mission support sections (for example, personnel, logistics, and engineering). The OSC-I also complied with that direction. As stated earlier, OSC-I initially cut unfilled positions, followed by positions that had recently, or soon would, become vacant.

By February 2013, as a result of negotiations between the U.S. Mission and the OSC-I, the CoM had directed and DoD had agreed to additional OSC-I reductions. That plan, which was agreed to after the OSC-I completed its updated mission analysis, called for reducing its personnel numbers to 170 by March 2013 and 125 by October 2013. Unlike initial reductions, later reductions cut more deeply into OSC-I ability to perform various functions. For instance, reducing from 170 to 125 billets decreased mission support personnel by 36 percent, from 28 to 18; and, total security cooperation personnel by 25 percent, from 128 to 96.

Besides certain elements of security assistance that are generally DOS-led but DoD executed, DoD is responsible for numerous other security cooperation programs (see Introduction). DoD-led security cooperation efforts typically utilize other DoD elements,[34] but Iraq's security situation precluded those elements from conducting activities they would have normally performed.

Coordination between DoD and DOS allowed OSC-I to conduct certain training and advisory activities that were considered a priority. These priorities included security cooperation activities such as the ministerial training that the OSC-I Senior Advisors' Group conducted and other efforts to improve Iraqi professional military education. Those priorities broadly supported Security Sector Reform, as well as promoted military-to-military relations. If carried out as planned, nearly 95 percent[35] of the total security cooperation billets to be eliminated would have supported those types of DoD-led security cooperation, versus FMS security assistance, mission efforts.

---

[34] Other DoD elements included combatant commands, like USCENTCOM, Military Services, and other OSD agencies.
[35] Of the total 32 security assistance and security cooperation billets eliminated, 30 supported DoD-led security cooperation rather than DOS-led security assistance efforts $(30 \div 32 = 93.75\%)$.

Impact of State Department-directed Staffing Decisions

On the current path, OSC-I could become an organization equipped to do security assistance with limited other security cooperation capability. For example, plans to reduce OSC-I from 170 to 125 total billets eliminate 32 overall security assistance and cooperation billets–30 who were primarily working on DoD-led security cooperation efforts.

> *OSC-I could become an organization equipped to do security assistance with limited other security cooperation capability*

Given these projected staff reductions, by the end of fiscal year 2013 OSC-I did not expect to be able to conduct security cooperation in the areas of Iraqi military leader development, professional military education, and senior staff training efforts. Those defense cooperation initiatives arguably supported the stated goal of promoting a strategic relationship with Iraq, but, over the course of this assessment, no DoD element, to include USCENTCOM, nor the CoM provided any systematic, mission based analysis that substantiated the rationale for possibly terminating them.

Premature elimination of OSC-I mission support personnel specialists, like logisticians and engineers, was another concern. Besides essential for transitioning DoD managed sites back to the government of Iraq, which were scheduled to begin in March 2013, these personnel provided critical mission support for the FMS security assistance program. As an example, one senior OSC-I logistician interviewed in November 2012 stated half of his total manpower was engaged in facilitating delivery of security assistance systems and material. That official expected any further personnel cuts to have "significant" impact. Overall, concerns were expressed to our team that OSC-I mission and support personnel reductions could impede it from performing important security cooperation activities in Iraq and potentially jeopardize accomplishment of related U.S. security policy objectives.

Besides that of the OSC-I, the methodologies used by others within DoD for assessing the impact of OSC-I personnel reductions and effectiveness were unclear. The NDAA for FY 2013 mandated Secretary of Defense reporting on OSC-I progress. An initial report was due 120 days from NDAA enactment with an update report due by September 30, 2013. Initial reporting required a description of measures of effectiveness for evaluating OSC-I activities, and a discussion of the process for using those measures of effectiveness to make determinations whether specific OSC-I activities should be expanded, altered, or terminated. Despite attempts to secure the initially required Secretary of Defense report information, as of June 2013 the DoD OIG had not been provided that information.[36]

Conclusion

The DOS process for determining OSC-I staffing reductions did not fully consider important DoD mission objectives and priorities, and the necessary resources required.

---

[36] See *NDAA (FY 2013) Mandatory Reporting*, Appendix C.

This occurred because the staffing reduction process did not follow established DOS "rightsizing" guidelines. Neither were these personnel cuts based on a joint, coordinated analysis of OSC-I resource needs in relation to an updated agreement concerning its operational goals and objectives. This consequently increases the potential that the OSC-I staff reductions included positions and personnel important to advancing security cooperation and security sector reform goals and objectives, which could inhibit promoting the end state development of a strong strategic relationship with Iraq.

Recommendations, Management Comments, and Our Response

Recommendation

2. Commander, U.S. Central Command, in coordination with Under Secretary of Defense for Policy, U.S. Chief of Mission in Iraq, and Chairman of the Joint Chiefs of Staff:

   2.a. identify and prioritize DoD security cooperation requirements needed to support updated Iraq Country Plan objectives, to include numbers of personnel and skill sets necessary to perform essential activities.

Management Comments

U.S. Central Command. Responding for the Commander, the U.S. Central Command Inspector General Executive Director agreed but did not provide information regarding whether they had identified and prioritized DoD security cooperation requirements or numbers of personnel and skill sets necessary to perform essential activities.

Joint Staff. In a consolidated Joint Staff response, the Deputy Director, Joint Education and Doctrine, Joint Staff J-7, stated that Joint Staff J-5 agreed and that J-5 coordination with the Under Secretary of Defense for Policy and U.S. Central Command resulted in the "Report on the Activities of the Office of Security Cooperation–Iraq" and U.S. Mission to Iraq "FY 2015 Mission Resource Request." Joint Staff provided copies of those documents in its response.

Our Response

U.S. Central Command comments were partially responsive. Although U.S. Central Command agreed with the recommendation, it did not state whether the command had identified and prioritized DoD security cooperation requirements or numbers of personnel and skill sets necessary to perform essential activities. However, information and documents forwarded by the Joint Staff, particularly the "Report on the Activities of the Office of Security Cooperation–Iraq," provided much of that information, except for the personnel skill sets required.

We request that U.S. Central Command respond to the final report by specifying the personnel skill sets required to perform the essential activities outlined in Section 4 of the "Report on the Activities of the Office of Security Cooperation–Iraq."

Joint Staff comments were fully responsive. We commend the Joint Staff for the completeness of its response and accompanying substantiating documentation. No further Joint Staff response is required.

Recommendation

2. Commander, U.S. Central Command, in coordination with Under Secretary of Defense for Policy, U.S. Chief of Mission in Iraq, and Chairman of the Joint Chiefs of Staff:

2.b. assess the risk to meeting theater and country-specific level planning objectives that result from various models to resource the Office of Security Cooperation–Iraq and other security cooperation requirements in Iraq.

Management Comments

U.S. Central Command. Responding for the Commander, the U.S. Central Command Inspector General Executive Director agreed and further stated that the command assessed moderate risk in meeting theater and country-specific level planning objectives with reduced personnel in the Office of Security Cooperation–Iraq. The Executive Director also stated there was ongoing deliberative interagency planning regarding the Office of Security Cooperation–Iraq scope and size, but that it was scheduled to reduce its personnel strength to 127 by September 30, 2013 and to 59 by FY 2015.

Joint Staff. In a consolidated Joint Staff response, the Deputy Director, Joint Education and Doctrine, Joint Staff, J-7, stated that Joint Staff J-5 agreed and that J-5 coordination with the Under Secretary of Defense for Policy and U.S. Central Command resulted in the "Report on the Activities of the Office of Security Cooperation–Iraq" and U.S. Mission to Iraq "FY 2015 Mission Resource Request." Joint Staff provided copies of those documents in its response.

Our Response

U.S. Central Command comments were partially responsive. Although U.S. Central Command agreed and stated that it had assessed moderate risk with an Office of Security Cooperation–Iraq comprised of reduced personnel, it did not state the specific number of personnel or inclusive dates for which that assessment applied. Due to the dynamic nature of the situation in Iraq, those details were essential to our assessment. While the Joint Staff response did not specifically address risk assessment, additional information provided was instructive in other ways.

Section 2 of the "Report on the Activities of the Office of Security Cooperation–Iraq" summarized Office of Security Cooperation–Iraq personnel and funding requirements essentially at its September 30, 2013 configuration and numbers of personnel, stating that level provided adequate capacity. It also, however, outlined a three-phase plan to transition Office of Security Cooperation–Iraq activity costs to Foreign Military Sales cases by FY 2015, transitioning primary responsibility for security cooperation to U.S. Central Command and reducing the Office of Security Cooperation–Iraq footprint to normalized levels—presumably around 59 personnel—by the end of FY 2014.

Although the report briefly mentioned using U.S. Central Command title 10 security cooperation programs, it lacked details about the extent and under what conditions traditional security cooperation authority, personnel, and program funding will be used to offset challenges and mitigate risk to mission accomplishment if efforts to transition costs to Foreign Military Sales case funding fall short.

In our judgment, Section 4 of that report presented a compelling case for sustaining the Office of Security Cooperation–Iraq at its currently projected September 30, 2013 personnel level throughout FY 2014, versus reducing it to 59 personnel by FY 2015. That section listed nearly a dozen critical security cooperation related activities that could not be effectively transitioned to traditional security assistance or cooperation authorities in the near-term and specified the number of personnel required to perform each activity. The total number of personnel to perform all activities basically equaled the September 30, 2013 personnel levels, versus the normalized levels projected by FY 2015. Another report section outlined an Office of Security Cooperation–Iraq assessment methodology, but it also lacked sufficient detail for our assessment purposes.

We therefore request that, in addition to the information requested for Recommendation 1.b., U.S. Central Command respond to the final report with specific information regarding its security cooperation mission risk assessment for Iraq. Response should include strategy-to-objective-to-task, associated troop-to-task, and risk to mission accomplishment analyses, as well as measures of effectiveness and actions U.S. Central Command has taken or plans to take to mitigate risk to security cooperation mission accomplishment in Iraq. Risk mitigation details should stipulate the extent and conditions under which U.S. Central Command intends, and is prepared and resourced, to implement traditional security cooperation authority, personnel, and program funding in Iraq. Overall, specifics should be sufficient to determine whether the methodology used to assess the effectiveness of Office of Security Cooperation–Iraq manning levels and degree of rigor used in applying that methodology adhered to current policy guidance and/or accepted best practices.

Joint Staff comments were responsive. We commend the Joint Staff for the completeness of its response and substantiating documentation. No further Joint Staff response is required.

Recommendation

2. Commander, U.S. Central Command, in coordination with Under Secretary of Defense for Policy, U.S. Chief of Mission in Iraq, and Chairman of the Joint Chiefs of Staff:

      2.c. advise Chairman of the Joint Chiefs of Staff of risk assessment results in order to inform the required Secretary of Defense reporting on the Office of Security Cooperation – Iraq mandated by the National Defense Authorization Act for FY 2013.

Management Comments

U.S. Central Command. Responding for the Commander, the U.S. Central Command Inspector General Executive Director agreed with the recommendation but did not state whether it had advised the Chairman of the Joint Chiefs of Staff of its risk assessment results.

Joint Staff. In a consolidated Joint Staff response, the Deputy Director, Joint Education and Doctrine, Joint Staff J-7, stated that Joint Staff J-5 agreed and that J-5 coordination with the Under Secretary of Defense for Policy and U.S. Central Command resulted in the "Report on the Activities of the Office of Security Cooperation–Iraq" and U.S. Mission to Iraq "FY 2015 Mission Resource Request." Joint Staff provided copies of those documents in its response.

Our Response

U.S. Central Command comments were non responsive. Specifically, the Inspector General Executive Director did not state whether U.S. Central Command advised the Chairman of the Joint Chiefs of Staff of its risk assessment results. Joint Staff response and additional information did not specifically address whether the "Report on the Activities of the Office of Security Cooperation–Iraq" was informed by U.S. Central Command risk assessment results.

We therefore request that U.S. Central Command provide comments to the final report, sufficient to determine whether it advised the Chairman of the Joint Chiefs of Staff of its risk assessment results. Response should specify what, if any, risk assessment results it reported, the period of time or specific date covered by those results, and when it advised the Chairman of the Joint Chiefs of Staff.

Joint Staff comments were responsive. No further Joint Staff response is required.

This Page Intentionally Left Blank

Observation 3. Office of Security Cooperation–Iraq Integration

Over a year after being declared fully operational capable, the OSC-I was not fully integrated into the U.S. Mission Iraq as a subordinate element, by physical location or through administrative processes.

This was caused by several factors.

- Physically:
  - the OSC-I size was over 50 percent larger than originally planned in 2009, in part because in 2010 the U.S. Mission formally requested that DoD perform additional activities that were delegated to the OSC-I in 2011; and,
  - the Baghdad Embassy Complex could not accommodate this increased number of personnel due to facility constraints.
- Administratively:
  - DoD did not clearly establish the OSC-I as a subordinate element of the U.S. Mission prior to the end of contingency operations as originally planned in 2011;
  - OSC-I personnel charged with establishing effective interagency relationships and operating procedures between the OSC-I and the U.S. Mission were insufficiently trained for their responsibilities; and,
  - The standard operating procedures (SOPs) to achieve full administrative and operating integration had not been prepared jointly by the embassy and the OSC-I.

Not completely integrating the OSC-I into the U.S. Mission detracted from overall unity of effort and contributed to DoD expending additional funding and personnel resources.

Applicable Criteria

U.S. Forces–Iraq Operation Order 11-01, Change 1, May 2011.

Memorandum of Agreement between Chief of Mission, U.S. Mission Iraq and Commander, U.S. Central Command Regarding Security Responsibility, signed January 2012.

DoD Instruction 5132.13, "Staffing of Security Cooperation Organizations (SCOs) and the Selection and Training of Security Cooperation Personnel," January 9, 2009.

DoD Directive 5105.65, "Defense Security Cooperation Agency," October 26, 2012.

DoD Directive 5105.75, "Department of Defense Operations at U.S. Embassies," December 21, 2007.

Defense Security Cooperation Agency Manual 5105.38-M, "Security Assistance Management Manual," updated through April 2013 (http://www.dsca.osd.mil/samm/).

Discussion

USCENTCOM–Chief of Mission Memorandum of Agreement

> *DoD-DOS Memorandum of Agreement caused OSC-I to appear as an independent element of the DoD instead of an integral part of the U.S. Mission*

DOS not receiving full funding to perform all required post-contingency responsibilities caused the Secretaries of Defense and State to agree DoD would assume responsibility for the security of its personnel in Iraq, as well as for funding and managing activities at certain sites there after the contingency ended. This also led to a memorandum of agreement between the Chief of Mission and USCENTCOM that codified OSC-I's direct and unique involvement in numerous major DoD and DOS activities.

The OSC-I was required to engage with DoD in order to sufficiently to execute this agreement and received DoD fiscal and other resources to accomplish it. Maintaining these ties with DoD may have delayed full integration with the U.S. Mission. But, the necessity for OSC-I maintaining this relationship with DoD during the transition in order to support DOS and the Mission apparently created the impression with some officials in DoD, as well as in DOS, that the OSC-I was and wanted to be a semi-independent element of DoD within Iraq instead of an integral part of the U.S. Mission. The explanation for OSC-I's unique role and resource requirements was not fully understood by or sufficiently explained within DoD or DOS, nor between OSC-I and the U.S. Mission. This led to inevitable organizational misunderstandings.

Size of the OSC-I

As the transition from a DoD to DOS lead security role in Iraq evolved, the OSC-I was delegated additional mission and support activities that increased its staff size. As a result of the DoD-DOS agreement, for example, the OSC-I assumed responsibility for several unique activities, such as the Force Protection Detachment (FPD), Joint Operations Center (JOC), Joint Intelligence Support Element (JISE), as well as an expanded OSC-I mission support staff.

In a standard SCO operating environment, some of these type activities as well as the execution of security cooperation would have been supported with personnel that were temporarily assigned and deployed under geographic combatant commander (Commander, USCENTCOM) authority. The OSC-I had to directly assume responsibility for all of these activities, which required more staff to be assigned to it. The staff size increased to a level that precluded it from fully integrating into the U.S. Mission because of limited office facilities and accommodations at the U.S. Embassy's main facility.

As the possibility of having a follow-on U.S. military force presence in Iraq diminished, the National Security Council (NSC) Deputies Committee approved an expanded OSC-I, which contributed to its inability to relocate to the Baghdad Embassy Complex. That NSC Deputies' approval occurred in late 2011, close to the time that the original planning timeline called for the OSC-I to achieve FOC, transition to CoM authority, and relocate to the BEC. While the USF-I OPORD directed integrating the OSC-I into the U.S. Mission by October 1, 2011, that planning was based on a smaller sized OSC-I.[37] Initially retaining most of the core OSC-I and its expanded functional mission support elements at EMASAA allowed for further growth, and the OSC-I assumed responsibility for even more activities and

> *The increased size of the OSC-I prevented complete physical integration into the U.S. Mission as was required*

elements that either directly supported the U.S. Mission or supplemented its capability. This included elements, like the Joint Intelligence Support Element and the OSC-I Joint Operations Center. The OSC-I consequently grew to over 260 total positions by December 2011, which BEC facilities could not then support.

Some of this increased growth in size was attributed to DoD requiring personnel that executed certain security cooperation efforts in Iraq to be assigned to the OSC-I. This was so that those DoD personnel would have the necessary level of formal privileges and immunities while performing their official duties (see Introduction and Observation 1). The physical separation, although OSC-I and the U.S. Mission compound were located across the street from one another (see Figure 4), facilitated OSC-I staffing to meet its obligations but further emphasized its perceived segregation from, rather than integration into, the U.S. Mission.

Figure 4. Separate U.S. Embassy and OSC-I Facilities

Source: DoD OIG SPO

Extended Mission Scope

OSC-I had additional security cooperation mission considerations than comparable organizations in other countries. OSC-I maintained a heightened security posture that

---

[37] See Introduction and Appendix C, *Size of the OSC-I.*

resembled an operational contingency headquarters, rather than a security cooperation partner. This occurred, at least in part, due to the DoD-DOS agreement regarding managing the respective sites. While the U.S. Mission possessed various support capabilities, one of its Regional Security Office (RSO) officials indicated that it lacked the capacity to support the OSC-I, particularly given required tempo of OSC-I activities and the distributed nature of its field sites (see Observation 2).

Some activities that the OSC-I conducted or supported did duplicate activities performed by the U.S. Mission. For example, OSC-I provided its own security and transportation in and around Iraq while the RSO of the U.S. Mission was also responsible for U.S. Mission security matters. Additionally, the OSC-I operated a separate Joint Operations Center that conducted operational coordination for OSC-I activities instead of relying on the U.S. Mission Tactical Operations Center at the Baghdad Embassy Complex operated by the RSO. This division of responsibilities, codified by the DoD-DOS agreement, was confusing to the OSC-I and sections within the U.S. Mission that were unaccustomed to a security cooperation organization performing these type functions.

The complexity of SCO mission responsibilities and relationships are challenging and involve multiple interagency lines of communication and authority, as depicted in Figure 5. Achieving unity of effort in regards to effectively implementing security cooperation in Iraq necessitated a fully coordinated and synchronized concept, plan, and set of activities, especially between the OSC-I and the U.S. Mission.

Figure 5. SCO Responsibilities and Relationships

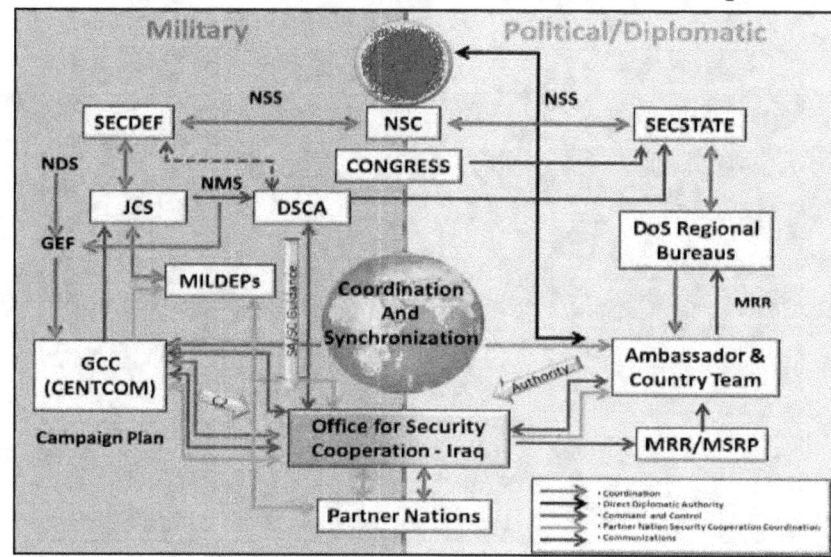

Source: DoD OIG SPO

Although physical integration of the OSC-I into the U.S. Mission was planned to occur by October 1, 2011, that had not been accomplished. In the interim, steps to administratively integrate the functions, like development of standardized procedures between the OSC-I and the U.S. Mission, were possible but, in November 2012 when the DoD OIG team visited Iraq, not occurring according to a deliberate plan or timetable.

Standard Operating Procedures

The OSC-I did not have a comprehensive plan, with a timetable, for developing essential standard operating procedures (see Appendix C). A previous DoD IG report (DODIG-2012-063) stated that neither USF-I nor OSC-I had established interagency SOPs essential to support complete integration into the U.S. Mission. In November 2012 when the DoD IG team most recently visited Iraq, the OSC-I did not have SOPs that directed crucial roles and activities with the U.S. Mission.

> *OSC-I had not published SOPs that would have assisted in integration and clarification of roles, responsibilities, and relationships*

Examples of missing required SOPs included standardized procedures that addressed:

- both administrative and operational functions;
- administrative responsibilities such as budgeting and cost sharing for sites and support services provided to OSC-I by the U.S. Embassy; and,
- force protection procedures at all DoD-managed field sites that required coordination with the Regional Security Officer.

Lack of clearly delineated responsibilities and procedures between the OSC-I and the U.S. Mission caused the OSC-I and U.S. Mission operations and relationship to be impaired (see Observation 1).

Required Training

> *OSC-I personnel lacked necessary training to provide foundational knowledge of the complexities of Security Cooperation*

Another obstacle to integration was that OSC-I personnel were not adequately trained. DoD Instruction 5132.13, "Staffing of Security Cooperation Organizations (SCOs) and the Selection and Training of Security Cooperation Personnel," states that assigned personnel shall receive military specialty training determined appropriate by the furnishing Military Service, and language, management, and other specific training as required by the Joint Table of Distribution (JTD)/Joint Manpower Process (JMP) and the personnel requisition.

It also states SCO personnel assigned security cooperation/assistance program management functions will attend the Security Cooperation Management–Overseas (SCM-O) course at the Defense Institute for Security Assistance Management (DISAM). Attendance at DISAM is mandatory, unless the course has been completed satisfactorily within the previous five years.

The situation in Iraq was recognized as unique and the OSC-I was required to deal with a number of operating challenges. DoD could have done more to support the efforts of the OSC-I by ensuring that more personnel were trained as required by DoD standards. The President's announcement to withdraw from Iraq by the end of 2011 occurred in early 2009, therefore DoD had a significant amount of time to ensure personnel assigned to the

OSC-I were trained as required by the time that it transitioned to CoM authority. Notwithstanding the online and mobile training teams that DoD did provide to the OSC-I, the magnitude of deviation from required training standards was notable and could have been avoided.

As of February 2013, the OSC-I reported that only 66 of 193 personnel reported trained had taken or received formal security cooperation training and only 38 had the required DISAM resident overseas course training. Meeting mandatory training requirements more fully would have provided the fundamentals for those OSC-I staff to effectively contribute to SCO operation and management. This was particularly important to differentiating between customary security cooperation activities and authorities and the special case that existed in Iraq.

The lack of proper training for the USF-I personnel that were assigned to the OSC-I as the transition to post-contingency occurred also contributed to a lack of OSC-I personnel understanding of and ability to execute security cooperation management and coordination under CoM and DOS authority. Moreover, the unique responsibilities delegated to the OSC-I by the DoD-DOS agreement for DoD and the OSC-I to provide resource support to the U.S. Mission may have led to further confusion as to the relationship between OSC-I and the U.S. Mission. This also may have impacted integration of the OSC-I into the U.S. Mission, causing integration efforts to be impeded.

Conclusion

By November 2012, over a year after being declared fully operational capable, the OSC-I was not fully integrated into the U.S. Mission and had separate facilities, security requirements, and administrative and operating procedures for day-to-day activities. DOS and DoD signed an MOA to ensure adequate support for both the U.S. Mission and OSC-I. Implementing that arrangement required significant direct OSC-I interaction with DoD. Having to interact more with DoD could have detracted the OSC-I from establishing closer relations with DOS and, although not intentionally, impeded development of an OSC-I that was fully integrated into the embassy.

In addition, the OSC-I and other DoD and DOS organizations did not establish a consensus or appropriate related guidance regarding the role and responsibilities of the OSC-I for post-2011. The lack of a joint DoD and DOS review of security cooperation activities to be taken by the OSC-I in support of U.S. policy goals undercut unity of effort. Also, because DoD, DOS, and the U.S. Mission did not agree on these activities or policy goals, OSC-I had to execute many day-to-day activities based on limited guidance and without a common understanding of its security cooperation activities (see Observation 1).

Lack of sufficiently trained and experienced OSC-I personnel inhibited establishing the fundamentals necessary for effective security cooperation organization operations and management under the authority of and within the integrated framework of the U.S. Mission. This included establishment of standard interagency operating procedures between the OSC-I and the U.S. Mission. Although physical integration was to occur by

October 31, 2013, an experienced and fully trained security cooperation cadre would have been more adept at improvising and implementing effective interim integration measures.

Full integration by OSC-I into the U.S. Mission was necessary for effecting transition of responsibilities for security at the DoD managed field sites and all support activities that were in the process of transitioning from DoD to DOS. Integration needed to be based on a common DoD and DOS understanding and acceptance of the scope of OSC-I security cooperation activities in order to achieve unity of effort. Insufficient integration also caused DoD to expend fiscal resources to accomplish those support and security cooperation activities which were delegated by DoD to the OSC-I to perform, but which DOS, the U.S. Mission, or other DoD elements may have been capable of performing.

Finally, integration without the support of a clearly defined set of security cooperation goals and objectives to be implemented by OSC-I, together with policy objectives for other key elements of the U.S. Mission, could impede effectively building a productive, long-term strategic partnership with Iraq, with the attendant consequences.

Recommendations, Management Comments, and Our Response

Added Recommendation

As a result of management comments and additional assessment efforts, we added a new Recommendation 3.c. to the final report for the Director, Cost Assessment and Program Evaluation (CAPE), directing that office to issue a resource management decision that supports transitioning the Office of Security Cooperation–Iraq to a Joint Table of Distribution personnel configuration.

Recommendation

> 3.a. Commander, U.S. Central Command, in coordination with:
>
> 3.a.(1) Under Secretary of Defense for Policy and Director of the Joint Staff, evaluate the Office of Security Cooperation–Iraq mission to validate personnel requirements necessary for coordinating and managing security cooperation activities and submit request for Joint Table of Distribution to the Joint Staff in order to permanently assign personnel to the Office of Security Cooperation–Iraq.

Management Comments

U.S. Central Command. Responding for the Commander, the U.S. Central Command Inspector General Executive Director stated that the Joint Staff validated the Office of Security Cooperation–Iraq Joint Table of Distribution requirements and the Vice Chairman of the Joint Chiefs of Staff endorsed the gain of 46 billets to U.S. Central Command's Joint Table of Distribution for the Office of Security Cooperation–Iraq. He also stated that U.S. Central Command continued to present the Office of the Secretary of

Defense with manpower requirements for resource decisions through the Program Budget Review and that, when the Office of the Secretary of Defense issued a resource management decision to transition the Office of Security Cooperation–Iraq to the Joint Table of Distribution, U.S. Central Command will add the billets to the Joint Table of Distribution and Services will add them to their documents and begin assigning permanent military/civilian personnel.

Joint Staff. In a consolidated Joint Staff response, the Deputy Director, Joint Education and Doctrine, Joint Staff J-7 stated Joint Staff J-1 agreed and that J-1 continued to support U.S. Central Command's efforts to transition the Office of Security Cooperation–Iraq to a permanent manning solution supported by a Joint Table of Distribution.

Defense Security Cooperation Agency. Although not required to comment, in a consolidated Joint Staff response, the Deputy Director, Joint Education and Doctrine, Joint Staff J-7, stated that the Defense Security Cooperation Agency agreed and that, in coordination with the Under Secretary of Defense for Policy and U.S. Central Command, it had reviewed and validated personnel requirements to establish and support 46 security assistance positions at the Office of Security Cooperation–Iraq.

Our Response

U.S. Central Command comments were responsive. We commend U.S. Central Command efforts to establish a Joint Table of Distribution for the Office of Security Cooperation–Iraq, which was important to providing stability and to establishing a baseline of personnel and activities to support U.S. national security objectives in Iraq. While providing 46 Joint Table of Distribution personnel to support security assistance programs that Department of Defense administered on behalf of Department of State, there was also an expected requirement for Joint Table of Distribution personnel to manage and coordinate broader security cooperation program activity as well. No further U.S. Central Command response is required.

In response to U.S. Central Command comments and to address that broader security cooperation personnel requirement, we acknowledged that the Office of the Secretary of Defense must issue a resource management decision and, therefore, added a new Recommendation 3.c. directed to the Director, Cost Assessment and Program Evaluation.

Joint Staff comments were responsive. No further Joint Staff response is required.

Recommendation

3.a. Commander, U.S. Central Command, in coordination with:

    3.a.(2) Director, Defense Security Cooperation Agency, and Chief, Office of Security Cooperation–Iraq, expedite obtaining the required training for all Office of Security Cooperation–Iraq personnel, as required by Department of Defense Directives and Instructions.

Management Comments

U.S. Central Command. Responding for the Commander, the U.S. Central Command Inspector General Executive Director agreed with the recommendation and stated that Security Cooperation Management training for personnel assigned to Security Cooperation Organizations was a high priority for U.S. Central Command. He also stated that the Services ensured incoming Office of Security Cooperation–Iraq personnel orders reflected necessary training, such as courses offered at the Defense Institute for Security Assistance Management. U.S. Central Command CCJ5-SC stated they will coordinate with the Office of Security Cooperation–Iraq, Defense Security Cooperation Agency, and the Defense Institute for Security Assistance Management to maximize the number of personnel that attend Defense Institute for Security Assistance Management courses before they arrived in Baghdad. They further stated that personnel who do not receive formal Security Cooperation Management training prior to reporting to the Office of Security Cooperation–Iraq were required to attend a course offered by that institute's mobile training team or utilize the institute's online training courses. CCJ5-SC also stated that, when billets are added to the Joint Table of Distribution, each position will reflect the required training requirements and that U.S. Central Command CCJ1 will state those requirements on its requests to fill the positions for the Services, in accordance with current directives and policies.

Defense Security Cooperation Agency. In a consolidated Joint Staff response, the Deputy Director, Joint Education and Doctrine, Joint Staff J-7 stated that the Defense Security Cooperation Agency agreed and that that agency had been coordinating with the Defense Institute for Security Assistance Management Commandant to expedite required training for incoming Office of Security Cooperation–Iraq personnel. They also stated that according to Defense Institute for Security Assistance Management Course rosters for the FY 2013 Overseas Course sessions, to date a total of 56 students were Office of Security Cooperation bound. Additionally, the Defense Institute for Security Cooperation Management sent a mobile training team to the Office of Security Cooperation–Iraq in March and September 2012 to conduct training for U.S. personnel only and that 102 personnel received training during those events. Even though the Defense Institute for Security Assistance Management did not know how many of those trained were still with the Office of Security Cooperation–Iraq, they stated that they were planning to send another mobile training team to Iraq in September 2013 to conduct additional training sessions for U.S. personnel.

Our Response

U.S. Central Command comments were responsive. We commend U.S. Central Command for its diligent monitoring of mandated training requirements in a very dynamic operating environment, taking actions to expedite training for Office of Security Cooperation–Iraq personnel, and utilizing mobile training teams to increase the training opportunity for personnel assigned to the Office of Security Cooperation–Iraq.

We request U.S. Central Command provide information regarding whether all assigned security assistance and security cooperation personnel have received required training, to include shortfalls of personnel not trained. We ask that U.S. Central Command coordinate with Defense Security Cooperation Agency regarding completion of in-country training scheduled for September 2013 to determine numbers of personnel trained and the type training provided (security cooperation or security assistance or both).

Recommendation

3.a. Commander, U.S. Central Command, in coordination with:

3.a.(3) Chief, Office of Security Cooperation–Iraq, establish a plan for transitioning responsibility for conducting security cooperation activities in Iraq, including the training and advisory activities referred to in the Foreign Assistance Act of 1961, as amended, to U.S. Central Command and other elements for execution.

Management Comments

U.S. Central Command. Responding for the Commander, the U.S. Central Command Inspector General Executive Director agreed and stated that there was currently deliberative interagency coordination to better define the longer-term U.S. strategy and inherent mission requirements. He also stated that the U.S. Mission in Iraq is on a glide path to assume a normalized configuration similar to other country teams and that Office of Security Cooperation–Iraq personnel were to completely transition to the U.S. Embassy compound by September 30, 2013, and assume a structure similar to other regional security cooperation offices.

Joint Staff. Although not required to comment, in a consolidated Joint Staff response, the Deputy Director, Joint Education and Doctrine, Joint Staff J-7, stated that Joint Staff J-5 agreed and that J-5 coordination with the Under Secretary of Defense for Policy and U.S. Central Command had resulted in the "Report on the Activities of the Office of Security Cooperation–Iraq" and the U.S. Mission to Iraq "FY 2015 Mission Resource Request." Joint Staff provided copies of those documents in its response.

Our Response

U.S. Central Command comments were partially responsive. Although U.S. Central Command agreed, comments did not sufficiently indicate the actions it had taken or planned to take to fully implement this recommendation.

While physical location may facilitate integration, it does not necessarily constitute complete integration by activity, membership, or coordination into the U.S. Mission in Iraq. The "Report on the Activities of the Office of Security Cooperation" provided by the Joint Staff was required by the National Defense Authorization Act of FY 2013 and outlined a plan to physically move Office of Security Cooperation–Iraq personnel from the Embassy Military Attaché and Security Assistance Annex (former Forward Operating Base Union III) to the Baghdad Embassy Complex. That report also included some details for transitioning responsibility for conducting security cooperation activities in

Iraq to U.S. Central Command by the end of FY 2014. Recognizing the difference between security cooperation and security assistance, it was understood that certain security assistance activities were not only conducted by but also wholly managed by the Department of State, while a number of security assistance programs were managed and conducted by Department of Defense in support of Department of State strategic objectives.

Full integration of the Office of Security Cooperation–Iraq was reported to be accomplished by the end of FY 2014, within a U.S. Mission in Iraq that would "assume a normalized mission similar to other country teams." Inconsistency existed in the dates to achieve full integration of activities that include all security cooperation programs, projects, and activities and security assistance programs managed and conducted by the Department of Defense.

We request that U. S. Central Command provide information when complete integration of the Office of Security Cooperation–Iraq has been achieved and when "normalization" has been achieved.

Recommendation

3.b. Chief, Office of Security Cooperation–Iraq, in coordination with the U.S. Chief of Mission in Iraq and Commander, U.S. Central Command, accelerate establishing requirements necessary for consolidating the Office of Security Cooperation–Iraq activities within the U.S. Mission Iraq, including development and publishing of standard operating procedures for all critical activities to facilitate full integration in minimum time.

Management Comments

Office of Security Cooperation–Iraq. In a consolidated response for the Commander, U.S. Central Command, the command Inspector General Executive Director stated that the Office of Security Cooperation–Iraq agreed and provided information regarding the Tikrit site closure and transition back to the government of Iraq. The response further stated that they were on track to complete site transition of Taji and Besmaya by September 30, 2013, and that they had transitioned 90 percent of Embassy Military Attaché and Security Assistance Annex office functions to the Baghdad Embassy Compound with a September 1, 2013 target to have functions and personnel transitioned. They also stated that security functions and responsibilities formalized in a security memorandum of agreement between the Office of Security Cooperation–Iraq and the U.S. Embassy in Baghdad were to take effect August 1, 2013. In addition, the Office of Security Cooperation–Iraq continues to formalize standard operating procedures between the Office of Security Cooperation–Iraq and the U.S. Embassy in Baghdad.

Joint Staff. Although not required to respond, in a consolidated Joint Staff response, the Deputy Director, Joint Education and Doctrine, Joint Staff J-7, stated that Joint Staff J-5 agreed and that J-5 coordinated with U.S. Central Command to provide information that resulted in the "Report on the Activities of the Office of Security Cooperation–Iraq."

Markings on that document, which Joint Staff included in its response, stated it was submitted pursuant to Public Law 112-239, the National Defense Authorization Act for FY 2013. That report showed the transition plan for Office of Security Cooperation–Iraq integration into the U.S. Mission in Iraq, with a projected completion date for physical integration of September 30, 2013. Further, the response stated that Joint Staff J-5 continued to communicate sufficient details about Office of Security Cooperation–Iraq capabilities, activities, and objectives to U.S. Country Team officials to enable their support, guidance, and oversight.

Our Response

The Office of Security Cooperation–Iraq comments were partially responsive. While agreeing and stating that transition of sites and personnel was to be complete by September 1, 2013, the Office of Security Cooperation–Iraq also stated that they continued to formalize standard operating procedures between the Office of Security Cooperation–Iraq and the U.S. Embassy in Baghdad.

We acknowledge the enormous effort by the Office of Security Cooperation–Iraq to transition the outlying sites and physically integrate its personnel into the Baghdad Embassy Complex while simultaneously assessing and restructuring the Office of Security Cooperation–Iraq organization.

We request the Office of Security Cooperation–Iraq provide additional specifics regarding the proposed list of standard operating procedures they plan to develop to govern their activities as a fully integrated office in the U.S. Mission Iraq, as well as a timeline indicating when those procedures will be completed and issued.

Recommendation (Added)

U.S. Central Command comments stated that when the Office of Secretary of Defense issued a resource management decision to transition the Office of Security Cooperation–Iraq to a Joint Table of Distribution, it will be able to add the billets to its Joint Table of Distribution and Services will add those requirements to their documents and begin assigning permanent military/civilian personnel.

We therefore added a new Recommendation 3.c. for implementation by the Office of the Secretary of Defense Cost Assessment and Program Evaluation.

3.c. Director, Cost Assessment and Program Evaluation, in coordination with the Under Secretary of Defense Comptroller, issue a resource management decision to support transition of the Office of Security Cooperation–Iraq to a Joint Table of Distribution that specifies personnel to manage, coordinate, and conduct the full range of security cooperation activities which encompasses those security assistance programs administered by Department of Defense.

Management Comments Required

We request that the Director, Cost Assessment and Program Evaluation provide comments on the final report.

This Page Intentionally Left Blank

Observation 4. Department of Defense Transition of Sites in Iraq

The OSC-I did not have the specialized personnel and equipment resources required to manage the closing down and transition to government of Iraq (GoI) control those field sites for which OSC-I has been responsible. DoD also did not have a comprehensive plan for enabling the transition of these sites.

The necessary resources were not available because the OSC-I was designed and staffed to perform security cooperation and security assistance activities, not to transition DoD managed sites to the GoI. Further, DoD had not yet committed all of the personnel and equipment resources needed to properly transition those sites to the GoI by the end of 2013.

Transitioning DoD managed sites without having the required specialized skills and capabilities available increased the risk of:

- not meeting established timelines for transitioning field sites, and
- compromising sensitive equipment items protected by U.S. law.

Further, diverting OSC-I personnel from their primary security assistance and security cooperation mission duties to perform site transition tasks would impede accomplishment of those primary responsibilities.

Applicable Criteria

DoD Directive 5132.03, "DoD Policy and Responsibilities Relating to Security Cooperation," October 24, 2008.

"National Defense Authorization Act for Fiscal Year 2013," Section 1211. P.L. 112-239, January 2, 2013.

Discussion

Background

By late 2010, the Department of State had not secured full congressional funding for all post-contingency operation activities in Iraq, and DoD agreed to take responsibility for funding and managing 6 of the 10 sites throughout Iraq. Since January 1, 2012, OSC-I had been authorized and funded to operate and maintain those six sites. The recent NDAA for FY 2013 included $508 million that funded the OSC-I efforts in Iraq and the security cooperation activities that it conducted, as well as operations at the various DoD managed field sites.

Complexity of Transitioning Sites

During 2012, DOS directed significant reductions of the U.S. Mission personnel and logistics which included the outlying sites. At the same time, the U.S. Mission made plans to accelerate the consolidation of its diplomatic and the DoD managed sites. In another action not directly related to DOS reductions, USCENTCOM also ordered OSC-I to plan for transitioning the outlying site of Kirkuk back to the GoI. The Kirkuk transition occurred over the course of several months and was completed in September 2012.

OSC-I transitioned Kirkuk before incurring the personnel reductions imposed by DOS and, therefore, it had more substantial resources to support the transitioning of that field site. U.S. Army further augmented that site transition effort with special logistics teams. Those special teams provided critical assistance in the performance of the required material inventory, packaging, and movement of USG equipment. Kirkuk also had a readily accessible airstrip capable of handling C-17 cargo aircraft, which was critical to ensuring a safe and responsible transition and retrograde of sensitive USG equipment.

> **Transitioning the remaining five DoD managed sites would be resource intensive**

Transitioning the remaining five DoD managed sites of Tikrit, Taji, Embassy Military Attaché and Security Assistance Annex (EMASAA, across the street from the main embassy compound in Baghdad), Umm Qasr, and Besmaya would be more resource intensive than Kirkuk. Coordinating the transition of those sites, especially by the end of 2013 as the then established timelines projected, would require additional personnel with special skills to conduct necessary logistics and other supporting activities, to include: transportation, multi-modal loadmasters, demilitarization supply experts, property accountability clerks, and intelligence personnel. However, DoD was generally reluctant to send its personnel into Iraq because of a lack of formal privileges and immunities, the DoD security concerns for its personnel, and Iraqi government sensitivities over the visibility of any increased U.S. military presence, other than the OSC-I.[38] It was therefore unclear whether these impediments would preclude deploying sufficient resources to complete the required tasks within the established timelines.

There were substantial amounts of USG material remaining at DoD managed field sites that must either be removed or disposed. As an example, members of the DoD IG team observed a large number of up-armored sport utility vehicles at Taji that had to be either returned to the U.S., or demilitarized and disposed of in-country. Existing U.S. technology export laws prohibited those articles and material from being transferred to the government of Iraq. On site disposal was an especially complicated task that required special authorization. Based on experience gained in transitioning Kirkuk, ground transportation in Iraq was a particularly limiting factor due to it being inconsistent and unreliable, which caused several delays in critical movements.

Another site transition factor that OSC-I officials expressed was considering the requirements for establishing follow-on FMS cases at the sites after the transition occurred if that was required. To effectively enable FMS case activity in those instances where it was required, site transitions had to be accomplished in a manner that accounted

---

[38] See *Privileges and Immunities*, Appendix C.

for GoI and FMS contractor requirements. This included effectively transitioning any available and necessary equipment to responsible parties, as well as ensuring required infrastructure elements at specific locations transitioned intact. Preserving and transitioning intact communications infrastructure was one such concern that OSC-I officials mentioned.

Site Transition Mission Analysis and Follow Through

Leveraging lessons learned from Kirkuk, OSC-I determined that site transition was a difficult undertaking beyond its capability to execute with existing resources. Given the Kirkuk experience it was recognized that transportation was a potentially limiting factor that needed to be carefully considered. The lessons learned review conducted for the Kirkuk transition recommended that future closures retain flexible options and plan for delays.

Based on its subsequent analysis, OSC-I formally requested additional resources from USCENTCOM. After validating that request for assistance, which included logistics teams and other necessary resources, USCENTCOM forwarded it to higher DoD echelons. There were indications that some site transition activity had occurred in response to that request. However, as of April 2013, DoD had not provided evidence of a comprehensive plan for transitioning the sites that it managed in Iraq back to the GoI.

In November 2012, OSC-I planners expected many activities at DoD managed sites to convert to follow-on, contractor based security assistance FMS cases. While several options for establishing FMS case activities were being explored at that time, site transition criteria remained unclear. As of April 2013, and lacking evidence of a comprehensive plan for transiting DoD-managed sites, it was unclear whether DoD had effectively considered the requirements or developed criteria for establishing follow-on FMS case activities at those site locations if establishing such a capability was required.

Conclusion

At the time the DoD IG team visited Iraq in November 2012, DoD primarily relied on OSC-I, a security cooperation organization under CoM authority, to transition the field sites that it managed. However, the OSC-I did not have the resources required to accomplish this mission on its own.

By April 2013, there were indications that some site transition activity had occurred, although it was unclear whether DoD had a comprehensive plan for transitioning the sites that it managed in Iraq back to the GoI. Effective transition was especially important for establishing follow-on FMS case activity when and where that was required.

Not providing OSC-I the required personnel and resources would greatly increase the risk that sensitive items protected by U.S. law could be compromised. It also increased the potential that established timelines for consolidating USG assets and personnel would not be met, which could impede the standup of follow-on, contractor-based FMS case activities at those locations after the transition to GoI control occurred. Further, diverting OSC-I personnel from their primary duties to perform site transition tasks increased the risk that achieving important security assistance and security cooperation efforts in Iraq would be delayed with possible negative consequences.

Recommendations, Management Comments, and Our Response

Recommendation

4.a. Commander, U.S. Central Command, in coordination with Chief, Office of Security Cooperation–Iraq, identify the requirements for fully transitioning Department of Defense designated sites in Iraq back to the government of Iraq, to include adjusting the transition timelines if necessary.

Management Comments

U.S. Central Command. Responding for the Commander, the U.S. Central Command Inspector General Executive Director agreed and further stated that it had issued a fragmentary order (FRAGO) regarding site transition in Iraq that provided the necessary direction, authority, money, and people to responsibly transition those sites back to the government of Iraq. That response provided additional information regarding the Office of Security Cooperation–Iraq request for additional resources, U.S. Central Command coordination and response to that request, and a copy of the referenced fragmentary order.

Joint Staff. Although not required to comment, in a consolidated Joint Staff response the Deputy Director, Joint Education and Doctrine, Joint Staff J-7, stated that Joint Staff J-4 agreed and that J-4 will continue to work with Department of Defense elements and U.S. Central Command to transition the sites in Iraq. The response stated that coordination with the Under Secretary of Defense for Policy and U.S. Central Command resulted in the "Report on the Activities of the Office of Security Cooperation–Iraq," which outlined the transition of sites in Iraq. Joint Staff included that report in its response.

Our Response

U.S. Central Command comments were fully responsive. We commend its efforts to identify and secure resources, as well as implement a whole-of-government approach to addressing challenges of transitioning the sites back to the government of Iraq. No further response is required.

Recommendation

4.b. Under Secretary of Defense for Policy, in coordination with Under Secretary of Defense for Acquisition, Technology, and Logistics and Chairman of the Joint Chiefs of Staff, take action to ensure necessary resources are available and allocated to U.S. Central Command in order to effectively transfer Department of Defense designated sites in Iraq back to the government of Iraq.

Management Comments

Under Secretary of Defense for Policy. In responding for the Under Secretary of Defense for Policy, the Principal Director for Middle East Policy agreed but did not further specify the action they had taken or planned to take to implement the recommendation.

Joint Staff. In a consolidated Joint Staff response the Deputy Director, Joint Education and Doctrine, Joint Staff J-7, stated that Joint Staff J-4 agreed and that J-4 will continue to work with Department of Defense elements and U.S. Central Command to transition the Department of Defense designated sites in Iraq. The response also stated that coordination with the Under Secretary of Defense for Policy and U.S. Central Command resulted in the "Report on the Activities of the Office of Security Cooperation–Iraq," which outlined the transition of sites in Iraq. Joint Staff included that report and other amplifying information in its response.

Our Response

The Under Secretary of Defense for Policy comments were partially responsive. Although agreeing, comments did not specify the actions they had taken or planned to take to ensure necessary resources were available and allocated to U.S. Central Command in order to effectively transfer Department of Defense designated sites in Iraq back to the government of Iraq. However, Joint Staff provided some of that additional information in its response and U.S. Central Command comments to Recommendation 4.a. provided the remaining necessary information. Therefore, no further Under Secretary of Defense for Policy response is required.

Joint Staff comments were fully responsive. We commend the Joint Staff for the completeness of its response and substantiating documentation. No further Joint Staff response is required.

This Page Intentionally Left Blank

Observation 5. Sufficiency of Joint Doctrine

A consolidated source of DoD joint doctrine did not exist to support the post-contingency transition of responsibility between DoD and DOS in Iraq, especially regarding the conduct of security cooperation activities.

DoD had not recognized the need for this doctrine before the transition of its lead responsibility from DoD to DOS in Iraq beginning in 2012. Joint doctrine at that time identified security cooperation planning and execution, but did not contain sufficient details to support post-contingency transition. Additionally, USCENTCOM had not systematically collected, analyzed, and integrated security cooperation or transition related lessons learned into the Joint Doctrine Development process as DoD directives require.

The lack of guidance regarding post-contingency transition of responsibilities between DoD and DOS impeded interagency efforts to fully integrate OSC-I capability into and achieve optimal synergy with the U.S. Mission in Iraq.

Applicable Criteria

DoD Directive 5132.03, "DoD Policy and Responsibilities Relating to Security Cooperation," October 24, 2008.

CJCS Instruction 3150.25E, "Joint Lessons Learned Program," April 20, 2012.

CJCS Instruction 5120.02C, "Joint Doctrine Development System," January 13, 2012.

Joint Publication 3-0, "Joint Operations," August 11, 2011.

Joint Publication 3-07, "Stability Operations," September 29, 2011.

Joint Publication 3-08, "Interorganizational Coordination During Joint Operations," June 24, 2011.

Joint Publication 5.0, "Joint Operation Planning," August 11, 2011.

Discussion

Importance of Joint Doctrine

Joint doctrine is important to training, educating, and developing U.S. military forces. It consists of fundamental principles that guide the employment of U.S. military forces in order to enhance the operational effectiveness of those forces. While not policy or strategy, joint doctrine is inherently linked to and informed by U.S. policy and serves to make policy and strategy effective in the application of U.S. military power. It represents what is taught, believed, and advocated as being right (that is, what works best). It standardizes terminology, training, relationships, responsibilities and processes among all U.S. forces to free joint force commanders and their staffs to focus efforts on solving the

51

strategic, operational, and tactical problems confronting them. These doctrinal shaping functions are especially important to achieving successful future activities.

Disparate Guidance

> *Current guidance governing security cooperation is located in several organizations within DoD*

Current guidance governing security cooperation programs and activities is currently managed and located within several organizations of the DoD. DoD Directives and Instructions provide policy and national strategic direction provides for guidance for security cooperation programs and activities but lack a common doctrinal approach to planning, assessing, and transitioning security cooperation, as well as common program, project, and activity descriptions. The Defense Security Cooperation Agency Manual 5105.38-M, "Security Assistance Management Manual (SAMM)," for instance, references security cooperation, but primarily describes security assistance and its procedural elements. Other guidance provides specific details regarding Security Cooperation Organization personnel identification, assignment, training, tour length, and responsibilities.

Existing joint planning doctrine does not effectively address transitioning between phases of a contingency operation or transitioning from a contingency to a post-contingency situation, especially one as unique as Iraq. For example, Joint Publication 5-0, "Joint Operation Planning," provides broad overarching guidance on the joint planning process but lacks a discussion on planning and assessing security and cooperation programs and activities in theater and country-level plans or whether or not to transition all, some, or none of them as the DoD-led contingency operation transitions to a DOS-led, Phase 0 situation. Joint Publication 3-0, "Doctrine for Joint Operations," establishes joint doctrine for directing, planning, and executing joint operations. That publication series primarily deals with conducting various types of joint operations. It also broadly discusses interorganizational coordination in unified action but provides little detail in terms of transitioning security cooperation activities from DoD to DOS.

Collectively, joint publications do not comprehensively encompass or address doctrine for transitioning to a post-contingency situation. They also lack sufficient guidance for effectively planning and executing security cooperation. For example, JP 3-07, "Stability Operations," addresses transitions, but it does not cover security cooperation or details for transitioning from a contingency to a post-contingency situation.

Transition Gaps

Joint doctrine does not effectively address and support DoD transitioning ongoing activities to DOS in a post-contingency or an uncertain environment. Joint doctrine has a six phase (Phase 0 through Phase V) contingency model, depicted in Figure 6, which helps explain this doctrinal gap. While spanning normal actions and activities, the model recognizes that all contingencies do not necessarily cycle through all of the six phases.

> *Joint doctrine does not effectively address and support DoD transitioning from contingency to post-contingency*

Joint doctrine describes the joint planning process for contingency operations but does not sufficiently address the transition between DoD and DOS that occurs following a contingency. As an earlier DoD Inspector General report indicated, JP 5-0, "Joint Operation Planning," mainly detailed those actions required to rapidly build up the military and transition it to a higher force employment status in response to an unfolding crisis, as would be experienced in transitioning from Phase 0 through Phase III for example. The transition from Phase III to Phase V is also explained, though to a lesser degree. Discussion of requirements to effectively transition from Phase V, Enable Civil Authority, back to Phase 0, Shape, as OSC-I experienced in Iraq, however, does not exist.

Figure 6. Contingency Phasing Model

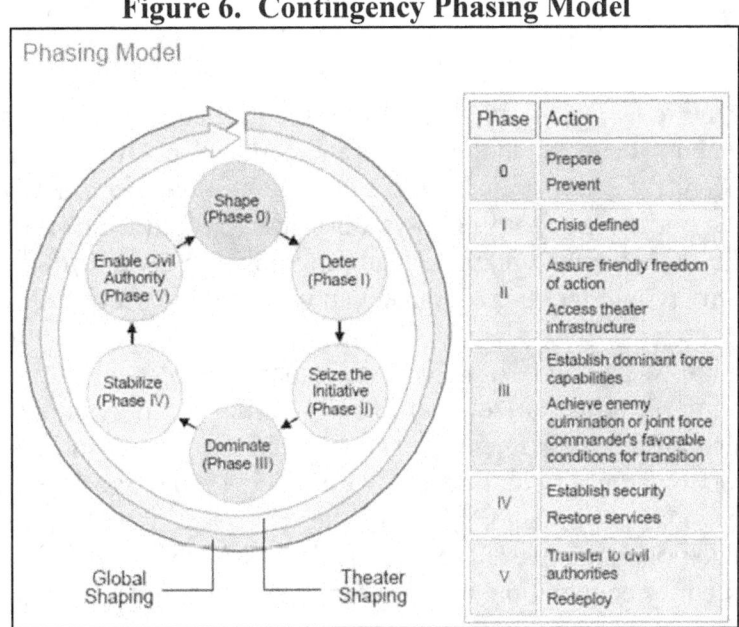

Source: JP 5-0.

During the time USF-I conducted drawdown and withdrawal activities, the lack of security cooperation transition guidance from Phase V to 0, contributed to post contingency issues. For instance, when higher echelons did not provide sufficient details regarding organizational requirements, functions, tasks, and activities, OSC-I had to organize and conduct activities it deemed necessary to accomplish its mission, as it was able to define it, based on previous existing USCENTCOM theater and country-specific planning guidance and identified in-country needs. This had to be accomplished in what one senior OSC-I official stated was an "authority-doctrine mismatch."

Another guidance shortcoming concerned a clear and sufficient understanding of the preparation and planning required for security cooperation. This gap contributed to differing views within DoD and between DoD and DOS regarding specific security cooperation roles and responsibilities. Interviews with OSC-I and USCENTCOM officials indicated a lack of consensus regarding the transition elements necessary for implementing the security cooperation mission. One senior OSC-I official provided a chart (see Introduction, Figure 3) illustrating some of the key issues OSC-I identified as requiring additional transition guidance. These included aspects such as authorities, funding, structure, and lines of communication. Lack of a unified position on these issues within DoD contributed to difficulties in agreeing on the OSC-I mission and resource requirements within the U.S. Mission.

Security cooperation planning also lacked a sufficiently forward looking planning horizon. In the current Joint Publication 3-0 series, all references to planning and executing security cooperation cite the Guidance for Employment of the Force (GEF), which generally follows the 2 year operational and contingency planning cycle. However, the planning of security cooperation Programs, Projects, and Activities (PPAs) necessitates a longer planning horizon in order to effectively compete for funding within the President's annual budgeting process by aligning requirements for implementing the plan with programmatic means.

To do that, the generic DoD planning horizon for security cooperation must effectively align the requirements identified in the theater and country-specific planning with programmatic means reflected in the Future Years Defense Program (FYDP) cycle. This extended planning horizon normally follows a 6-year cycle and would assist in synchronizing the DOS resource planning and programming cycle with the DoD security cooperation activity requirements, programs, and implementing resources.

The situation in Iraq was a good example of the importance of establishing a longer security cooperation planning horizon, particularly during complex interagency transition efforts. At the time of this assessment, DoD continued to primarily utilize the special congressional training authority in the NDAA for FY 2013 and overseas contingency operations funding in Iraq through FY 2013. After FY 2013, however, USCENTCOM security cooperation planning needed to effectively link its intended future activities to the established security cooperation programs and funding sources necessary to achieve longer-term objectives in Iraq. It was not evident that this had been accomplished and, therefore, uncertain whether sufficient programmatic security cooperation resources would be made available to ensure those objectives would be achieved.

Importance of Lessons Learned

Lessons learned are important to developing and refining joint doctrine. Besides benefiting current operations, identifying doctrinal gaps helps improve future performance. The OSC-I established a relationship with the Center for Army Lessons Learned (CALL) to collect and analyze lessons learned at their level. The CALL used the results of their analysis to publish and update a formal handbook entitled "Senior Leader's Guide to Transition Planning." USCENTCOM was aware of those lessons learned efforts but not directly involved in that process. Otherwise, USCENTCOM did not systematically collect, analyze, and submit security cooperation or Iraq transition-related lessons learned, as required by CJCS instructions. For instance, USCENTCOM interviewees stated that lessons from across the various USCENTCOM headquarter sections were not being collected, analyzed, and consolidated for submission into the Joint Doctrine Development Process. It was unclear why this had not occurred. Joint

Staff doctrine officials confirmed they had not received security cooperation or Iraq transition related lessons learned from USCENTCOM.

Nevertheless, Joint Staff doctrine officials were continuing with the joint doctrine development process based on security cooperation-related lessons learned inputs from the Joint Doctrine Development Community (JDDC), which consists of representatives from combatant commands, Services, and Combat Support Agencies. As of February 2013, those sources mainly consisted of organizational

> *Transitioning from stability operations to security cooperation activities require consolidated doctrine*

representatives that had attended the November 2012 50th Joint Doctrine Planners Conference. That forum, which identified a gap in doctrine involving security cooperation, unanimously recommended developing a new JP 3-XX "Joint Support to Security Cooperation." However, those joint doctrine officials that we interviewed also indicated that inputs received up until that point were insufficient to support developing new or updating existing doctrine.[39]

Conclusion

The lack of consolidated joint doctrine regarding security cooperation and the post-contingency transition of responsibility between DoD and DOS inhibited synergy between other USG and DoD efforts in Iraq. Though joint doctrine mentioned security cooperation in numerous instances, it lacked important details and was therefore incomplete. The USCENTCOM had not contributed to establishing sufficient doctrinal input since it had not ensured relevant lessons learned from the Iraq transition were systematically collected, analyzed, and sponsored into the Joint Doctrine Development process, as required by CJCS Instruction 5120.02C, "Joint Doctrine Development System."

While these shortfalls contributed to a lack of understanding on how to properly integrate OSC-I capability to achieve optimal synergy with the U.S. Mission in Iraq, developing improved joint doctrine also has longer-term importance to the U.S. military. Updated security cooperation and related transition doctrine and guidance are required to inform and shape U.S. force development efforts, such as training and leader development, as well as generating force requirements and capabilities for future post-contingency operational transitions.

Transitioning from stability operations to security cooperation activities will be especially important to future transitions as it was and is in Iraq. A single source DoD publication in this regard would assist in consolidating important information that is now dispersed throughout numerous publications. It would also assist in clarifying relationships between various interagency partners and programs, which could be of significant benefit to the upcoming transition and post-contingency security cooperation efforts in Afghanistan.

---

[39] See *Joint Doctrine Development*, Appendix C.

Recommendations, Management Comments, and Our Response

Recommendation

5.a. Commander, U.S. Central Command, in coordination with Under Secretary of Defense for Policy and Director, Joint Force Development, Joint Staff J7:

      5.a.(1) initiate a recommendation for fast track development of doctrine that covers transition of security cooperation and other responsibilities between the Department of Defense and Department of State in the post-contingency environment as has been occurring in Iraq beginning in 2011 and will need to be applied in Afghanistan post-2014.

Management Comments

U.S. Central Command. Responding for the Commander, the U.S. Central Command Inspector General Executive Director agreed and further stated that, given appropriate lead times, the command could support the joint doctrine development process. The response also stated any joint doctrine developed would be too late to inform transition planning for Afghanistan because those plans were scheduled to be published in the first quarter of FY 2014–1 year out from execution, as lessons from Iraq suggested was appropriate. The Executive Director also stated that concurrently supporting joint doctrine development while planning for the Afghanistan transition would unacceptably tax the command's limited planning resources.

Joint Force Development, Joint Staff J-7. Responding for the Director, Joint Force Development, Joint Staff J-7, the Deputy Director, Joint Education and Doctrine, Joint Staff J-7, agreed with the recommendation and further stated that, in accordance with Chairman of the Joint Chiefs of Staff Instruction 5120.02C, the Joint Staff, combatant commands, Military Services, and the Under Secretary of Defense for Policy were reviewing the J-7 directed Preliminary Coordination Program Directive for a new joint publication. He additionally stated that J-7 continued to work with specialized centers of excellence to incorporate lessons learned into that new joint publication, as well as other applicable joint publications.

Our Response

U.S. Central Command comments were partially responsive. Although the command's Inspector General Executive Director agreed and stated the command could support joint doctrine development, he did not specify the actions U.S. Central Command had taken or planned to take to implement the recommendation. In addition, Recommendation 5.a.(1) was not intended to solely address the actions leading up to a formal transition from military- to civilian-led authority as a military contingency winds down. While that is a consideration, its main intent is to address the transitional state and challenges that endure *after* that major transition event occurs. Specifically, it is to ensure joint doctrine effectively informs practitioners of the incremental transition of responsibilities that continues to occur between Department of Defense and Department of State until a more normalized state and set of political/military relationships can be secured.

Using the 1 year advance planning timelines from Iraq cited by U.S. Central Command, fast track development of joint doctrine was warranted and would be in time to address post-2014 transition challenges in Afghanistan because that period was then projected to extend to 2018 and beyond. Comments by U.S. Central Command to Recommendation 1.b. substantiated that it was projecting to continually update its theater- and Iraq-specific security cooperation plans following the major transition from military- to civilian-led authority in Iraq (see Appendix F). It was reasonable to expect that similar post-contingency planning will be performed for Afghanistan after 2014.

Given this clarification, we request that U.S. Central Command reevaluate its comments and provide a response to the final report that includes specific actions it has taken or plans to take to implement this recommendation. In light of the competing demands on limited planning resources, we encourage U.S. Central Command to seek external support to fulfill its Chairman of the Joint Chiefs of Staff-directed joint doctrine development responsibilities and suggest soliciting external support from such organizations as the Joint Staff J-7 Joint Center for Operational Analysis.

Deputy Director, Joint Education and Doctrine, Joint Staff J-7, comments were fully responsive. We commend the Joint Staff for the completeness of its response and proactive approach to expedited development of joint security cooperation doctrine. No further Joint Staff J-7 response is required.

Recommendation

5.a. Commander, U. S. Central Command, in coordination with Under Secretary of Defense for Policy, and Director, Joint Force Development, Joint Staff J7:

     5.a.(2) systematically compile and formally submit joint lessons learned to ensure observations and insights emerging from ongoing post-contingency transition activities are captured and incorporated into joint doctrine.

Management Comments

U.S. Central Command. Responding for the Commander, the U.S. Central Command Inspector General Executive Director agreed but did not specify what actions the command had taken or planned to take to implement this recommendation.

Joint Force Development, Joint Staff J-7. Responding for the Director, Joint Force Development, Joint Staff J-7; the Deputy Director, Joint Education and Doctrine, Joint Staff J-7, agreed and further stated that, in accordance with Chairman of the Joint Chiefs of Staff Instruction 5120.02C, the Joint Staff, combatant commands, Military Services, and the Under Secretary of Defense for Policy were reviewing the J-7 directed Preliminary Coordination Program Directive for a new joint publication and that Joint Staff J-7 continued to work with other specialized centers of excellence to incorporate lessons learned into that new joint publication, as well as other applicable joint publications.

Our Response

U.S. Central Command comments were non responsive. The Inspector General Executive Director did not state specific actions U.S. Central Command has taken or plans to take to implement this recommendation.

We request U.S. Central Command provide comments to the final report that specify what actions it has taken or plans to take to ensure observations and insights emerging from ongoing post-contingency transition activities are effectively captured and incorporated into joint doctrine in a timely manner. Besides planning and other activities leading up to the transition from military- to civilian-led authority, this should specifically address post-contingency planning and other activities that occur immediately after the contingency period winds down and continues until a more normalized state is achieved. It is particularly important that, besides lessons learned from field organizations, lessons from across the combatant command headquarters be systematically compiled, submitted, and incorporated into joint doctrine.

Joint Force Development, Joint Staff J-7, comments were fully responsive. We commend the Joint Staff J-7 for the completeness of its response and proactive approach to expedited development of joint security cooperation doctrine. No further Joint Staff J-7 response is required.

Recommendation

5.a. Commander, U. S. Central Command, in coordination with Under Secretary of Defense for Policy and Director, Joint Force Development, Joint Staff J7:

5.a.(3) review and recommend changes to appropriate joint doctrine publications to ensure they effectively reflect the doctrinal aspects of planning for and conducting security cooperation and other transition activities in a post-contingency environment.

Management Comments

U.S. Central Command. Responding for the Commander, the U.S. Central Command Inspector General Executive Director agreed but did not specify what actions the command had taken or planned to take to implement this recommendation.

Joint Force Development, Joint Staff J-7. Responding for the Director, Joint Force Development, Joint Staff J-7; the Deputy Director, Joint Education and Doctrine, Joint Staff J-7 agreed. He further stated that, in accordance with Chairman of the Joint Chiefs of Staff Instruction 5120.02C, the Joint Staff, combatant commands, Military Services, and the Under Secretary of Defense for Policy were reviewing the J-7 directed Preliminary Coordination Program Directive for a new joint publication and that J-7 continued to work with other specialized centers of excellence to incorporate lessons learned into that new publication, as well as other applicable joint publications.

Our Response

U.S. Central Command comments were non responsive. The Inspector General Executive Director did not state specific action U.S. Central Command has taken or plans to take to implement this recommendation.

We request U.S. Central Command provide comments to the final report specifying what actions it has taken or plans to take to review and recommend changes to joint doctrine publications to ensure they effectively reflect the doctrinal aspects of planning for and conducting security cooperation and other transition activities in a post-contingency environment. Besides the planning and other activities leading up to the transition from military-to civilian-led authority, this should specifically address post-contingency planning and other activities that occur immediately after the contingency period winds down and continues until a more normalized state is achieved. The response should also address how U.S. Central Command plans to systematically compile, submit, and ensure lessons learned from across its headquarter elements are incorporated into joint doctrine.

Joint Force Development, Joint Staff J-7 comments were fully responsive. We commend the Joint Staff J-7 for the completeness of its response and proactive approach to expedited development of joint security cooperation doctrine. No further Joint Staff J-7 response is required.

Recommendation

5.b. Director, Joint Force Development, Joint Staff J-7, in accordance with Chairman of the Joint Chiefs of Staff Instruction 5120.02C and in coordination with Under Secretary of Defense for Policy and Commander, U.S. Central Command, review joint doctrine and provide recommendations for consolidating emerging information from the situation in Iraq as it relates to conducting security cooperation and transitioning responsibilities between Department of Defense and other departments in complex, uncertain post-contingency security environments.

Management Comments

Joint Force Development, Joint Staff J-7. Responding for the Director, Joint Force Development, Joint Staff J-7; the Deputy Director, Joint Education and Doctrine, Joint Staff J-7 agreed and further stated that, in accordance with Chairman of the Joint Staff Instruction 5120.02C, a thorough review of applicable joint doctrine was conducted, resulting in the development of JP 3-XX, Military Support to Security Cooperation. The Deputy Director stated J-7 will incorporate the National Defense University Center for Complex Operations "Security Transition Planning Doctrine Proposal" and the U.S. Army Center for Army Lessons Learned "Senior Leader's Guide to Transition Planning" lessons learned into the new JP 3-XX. Moreover, the Deputy Director stated that lessons learned from security cooperation and transitioning responsibilities will be infused in applicable existing joint doctrine during programmed revision cycles.

Our Response

Joint Staff J-7 comments were partially responsive. We commend the Joint Staff J-7 for its proactive approach to expedited development of joint security cooperation doctrine. However, the response did not indicate a timeframe for when JP 3-XX would be completed or when lessons learned would be infused into existing joint doctrine. We therefore request Joint Staff J-7 provide a copy of the referenced National Defense University Center for Complex Operations document and, when completed, Joint Publication 3-XX, as well as a schedule of the programmed revision cycles for Joint Publications 3-0, 3-07, 3-08, and 5-0.

Appendix A. Scope, Methodology, and Acronyms

We conducted this assessment from August 2012 to June 2013 in accordance with the standards published in the *Quality Standards for Inspection and Evaluation*. We planned and performed the assessment to obtain sufficient and appropriate evidence to provide a reasonable basis for our observations and conclusions based on our assessment objectives. We believe that the evidence obtained provides a reasonable basis for our findings and conclusions based on our assessment objectives.

In the U.S., we met with personnel from the Defense Security Cooperation Agency; the Office of the Under Secretary of Defense for Policy; the Office of the Under Secretary of Defense (Comptroller)/Chief Financial Officer; Joint Chiefs of Staff J5 and J7 Directorates; and U.S. Central Command. In Iraq, we visited Forward Operating Base Union III (now the Embassy Military Attaché and Security Assistance Annex); the U.S. Embassy in Baghdad; and Contingency Operating Sites Besmaya and Taji. At these locations we observed current operations and we met with U.S. and Iraqi leaders and managers at various levels, ranging from general officers, to staff officers, to senior embassy personnel involved in and responsible for training, planning, and implementation of security assistance and security cooperation transition activities in Iraq.

We reviewed documents such as Federal laws and regulations, including the National Defense Authorization Act, Chairman of the Joint Chiefs of Staff instructions, DoD directives and instructions, and appropriate USCENTCOM plans and guidance applicable to the assessment objectives. We also collected and reviewed supporting documentation.

Use of Computer-Processed Data

We did not use computer-processed data to perform this assessment.

Use of Technical Assistance

We did not use Technical Assistance to perform this assessment.

Acronyms Used in this Report

The following is a list of the acronyms used in this report.

ACSA	Acquisition and Cross Servicing Agreement
AECA	Arms Export Control Act
ARCENT	U.S. Army Forces, U.S. Central Command
BEC	Baghdad Embassy Complex
CALL	Center for Army Lessons Learned
CCIF	Combatant Commander Initiative Fund
CJCS	Chairman of the Joint Chiefs of Staff
CoM	Chief of Mission
CTFP	Combating Terrorism Fellowship Program

DSCA	Defense Security Cooperation Agency
DoD OIG	Department of Defense Office of Inspector General
DOS	Department of State
DOS OIG	Department of State Office of Inspector General
DCG A&T	USF-I Deputy Commanding General for Advising and Training
DCCEP	Developing Country Combined Exercise Program
DCS	Direct Commercial Sales
DISAM	Defense Institute for Security Assistance Management
DSCA	Defense Security Cooperation Agency
EMASAA	Embassy Military Attaché and Security Assistance Annex
EUM	End-use Monitoring
E-IMET	Extended-International Military and Education Training
FAA	Foreign Assistance Act
FMFP	Foreign Military Finance Program
FMS	Foreign Military Sales
FOAA	Foreign Operations and Appropriations Act
FOC	Full Operating Capability
FPD	Force Protection Detachment
FYDP	Future Years Defense Program
GCC	Geographic Combatant Command
GoI	Government of Iraq
IOC	Initial Operating Capability
IMET	International Military Education Training
ISF	Iraqi Security Forces
ISFF	Iraq Security Forces Fund
JCET	Joint Combined Exchange Training
JDDC	Joint Doctrine Development Community
JISE	Joint Intelligence Support Element
JOC	Joint Operations Center
JTD/JMP	Joint Table of Distribution/Joint Manpower Process
LOA	Letter of Offer and Acceptance
MAP	Military Assistance Programs
MILDEP	Military Department
MET	Mobile Education Team
MOA	Memorandum of Agreement
MoD	Ministry of Defense
MOU	Memorandum of Understanding
MRPAT	Mobile Redistribution Property Assistance Team
MTT	Mobile Training Team
NDAA	National Defense Authorization Act
NSC	National Security Council
ODA	Office of Defense Attaché
OIF	Operation Iraqi Freedom
OSC-I	Office of Security Cooperation–Iraq
OND	Operation New Dawn
OPORD	Operations Order

PPA	Programs, Projects, Activities
PME	Professional Military Education
RSI	Rationalization, Standardization, and Interoperability
RSO	Regional Security Officer
SA	Security Assistance
SAMM	Security Assistance Management Manual
SC	Security Cooperation
SCM-O	Security Cooperation Management–Overseas
SCO	Security Cooperation Organization
SDO/DATT	Senior Defense Official/Defense Attaché
SOP	Standard Operating Procedure
SSR	Security Sector Reform
TCA	Traditional Commander Activities
USAID	U.S. Agency for International Development
USCENTCOM	U.S. Central Command
U.S.C.	United States Code
USEMB-B	United States Embassy–Baghdad
USF-I	United States Forces–Iraq
USG	United States Government

This Page Intentionally Left Blank

Appendix B. Summary of Prior Coverage

During the last three years, Congress, the Commission on Wartime Contracting in Iraq and Afghanistan, the Government Accountability Office, the Department of Defense Inspector General, and the Department of State Inspector General issued reports discussing topics related to the transition of the security assistance mission from the DoD to the Department of State.

Commission on Wartime Contracting reports can be accessed over the Internet at www.wartimecontracting.gov. Unrestricted Government Accountability Office reports can be accessed over the Internet at www.gao.gov. Unrestricted DoD IG reports can be accessed over the Internet at http://www.dodig.mil/audit/reports or at http://www.dodig.mil/spo/reports. Department of State Inspector General reports can be accessed over the Internet at http://oig.state.gov.

Some of the prior coverage we used in preparing this report included:

Congressionally Initiated Reports

"Iraq: The Transition From a Military Mission to a Civilian-Led Effort," A Report to the Members of the Committee on Foreign Relations, United States Senate, One Hundred Twelfth Congress, First Session, January, 2011.

Commission on Wartime Contracting in Iraq and Afghanistan

CWC Special Report 4, Follow-up Report on Preparing for Post—2011 U.S. Presence in Iraq, "Iraq—a forgotten mission?" March, 2011.

GAO

GAO-13-84, "Security Assistance: DOD's Ongoing Reforms Address Some Challenges, but Additional Information Is Needed to Further Enhance Program Management," November 2012

GAO-12-317, "Embassy Management: State Department and Other Agencies Should Further Explore Opportunities to Save Administrative Costs Overseas," January 2012

GAO-11-774, "Iraq Drawdown: Opportunities Exist to Improve Equipment Visibility, Contractor Demobilization, and Clarity of Post-2011 DoD Role," September 2011.

GAO-11-419T, "Foreign Operations: Key Issues for Congressional Oversight," March 2011.

Department of Defense Inspector General

DODIG-2012-063, Special Plans and Operations, "Assessment of the DoD Establishment of the Office of Security Cooperation–Iraq," March 16, 2012

SPO-2011-008, Special Plans and Operations, "Assessment of Planning for Transitioning the Security Assistance Mission in Iraq from Department of Defense to Department of State Authority," August 25, 2011

Department of State Inspector General

MERO-I-11-08, Middle East Regional Office, "Department of State Planning for the Transition to a Civilian-led Mission in Iraq," May 2011.

MERO-A-09-10, Middle East Regional Office, "Performance Evaluation of Embassy Baghdad's Transition Planning for a Reduced United States Military Presence in Iraq," August 2009.

Appendix C. Glossary

This Appendix provides definitions of terms used in this report.

Combatant Commander Initiative Fund. As detailed in 10 U.S.C. 166a, the Chairman of the Joint Chiefs of Staff (CJCS) may provide funds to the commander of a combatant command, upon the request of the commander, or, with respect to a geographic area or areas not within the area of responsibility of a commander of a combatant command, to an officer designated by the CJCS for such purpose. The Chairman may provide such funds for any of the following activities: force training; contingencies; selected operations; command and control; joint exercises (including activities of participating foreign countries); humanitarian and civic assistance, in coordination with the relevant chief of mission to the extent practicable, to include urgent and unanticipated humanitarian relief and reconstruction assistance; military education and training to military and related civilian personnel of foreign countries (including transportation, translation, and administrative expenses); personnel expenses of defense personnel for bilateral or regional cooperation programs; force protection; and joint warfighting capabilities.

Foreign Military Sales Program. The Foreign Military Sales Program is that part of security assistance conducted using formal agreements between the U.S. Government and an authorized foreign purchaser or international organization.

Joint Doctrine Development. Joint Staff reported that they had identified and were planning to address security cooperation doctrine gaps. The Joint Doctrine Development Community noticed key relationships among the topics of Security Force Assistance (SFA), Foreign Internal Defense (FID), Security Sector Reform (SSR), Security Cooperation (SC) and Security Assistance (SA), along with the lack of a document that "pulls it all together." As reported by the 50th Joint Doctrine Planners Conference: within the JP 3-0 series SFA is mentioned in 11 publications, SC in 49, and FID in 29, along with a lengthy discussion of SFA in JP 3-22 (FID). This dispersion of topics in so many different publications makes it very difficult to find specific subjects regarding SC. Conference results also noted the difference between the ways and means regarding SC and that JP 3-0 did not clearly state the relationship between SA and SC.

Memorandums of Agreement and Understanding. In 1986, Congress passed The Omnibus Diplomatic Security and Antiterrorism Act of 1986 that expressed requirements for increased security by all overseas missions and identified interagency coordination needed to accomplish those tasks. In 1997, in response to Khobar towers bombing, a memorandum of understanding (MOU) was signed by the Department of State and Department of Defense which further identified State requirements that would be accomplished by DoD regarding Marine Security Guards and other physical security activities at overseas posts. Then, in 2004, a memorandum of agreement between Commander, U.S. Central Command and Chief of Mission, U.S. Mission Iraq, was signed to delineate security responsibilities between the two agencies in Iraq during the first years of the Iraq war. That agreement was in accordance with the MOU of 1997 and described DoD Elements and Personnel Under the Security Responsibility of the Chief of Mission in "Annex A" and DoD Elements and Personnel Under the Security and Responsibility of the Combatant Commander in "Annex B." In this agreement, "Annex C" was introduced to provide authority for Security of Non-DoD USG Personnel. It specified categories of personnel to be provided security located at certain facilities under the responsibility of Commander, USCENTCOM and CoM over personnel in Iraq while operating or embedded with operational forces. In 2012, a modified MOA between the Commander, USCENTCOM and CoM, U.S. Mission Iraq was signed maintaining "Annex C" and identifying OSC-I and other DoD elements as the special case to security of personnel and facilities in Iraq.

National Defense Authorization Act (NDAA) FY 2013 Mandatory Reporting. Section 1211 of the NDAA for FY 2013 included mandatory reporting by the Secretary of Defense. In general, not later than 120 days after the Act was enacted, the Secretary of Defense, in consultation with the Secretary of State, was to submit to congressional committees a report on the activities of the Office of Security Cooperation in Iraq. Matters that the report directed were to be included: (A) A description, in unclassified form (but a classified annex if appropriate), of any capability gaps in the security forces of Iraq, including capability gaps relating to intelligence matters, protection of Iraq airspace, and logistics and maintenance; (B) A description of the extent, if any, to which the programs of the Office of Security Cooperation in Iraq, in conjunction with other United States programs such as the Foreign Military Financing program, the Foreign Military Sales program, and joint training exercises, will address the capability gaps described in subparagraph (A) if the government of Iraq requests assistance in addressing such capability gaps; (C) A detailed discussion of the current manpower, budget, and authorities of the Office of Security Cooperation in Iraq; (D) A detailed plan for the transition of the costs of the activities of the Office of Security Cooperation in Iraq to Foreign Military Sales case funding by September 30, 2014, and a detailed description of the planned manpower, budget, and authorities of the Office to implement such a plan; (E) A description of existing authorities available to be used to cover the costs of training the Iraqi Security Forces, including a list of specific training activities and number of associated personnel that the Secretary of Defense determines cannot be conducted under any existing authority not provided by this section; and, (F) A description of those measures of effectiveness that will be used to evaluate the activities of the Office of Security Cooperation in Iraq and a discussion of the process that will use those measures of effectiveness to make determinations if specific activities of the Office should be expanded, altered, or terminated. Not later than September 30, 2013, the Secretary of Defense, in consultation with the Secretary of State, was to submit to congressional committees an update of the initial 120 day report, including a description of any changes to any specific element or process described in elements (A) through (F) above.

OSC-I Lines of Operation. The four lines of operation (and respective exemplar activities) within the OSC-I strategy framework were: 1) Modernize [Note: This later changed to Force Generation] (Material Fielded, Sustainment Institutionalized, Facilities Upgraded); 2) Train (Institutional Improved, Operational Enabled, Interagency

Integrated); 3) Professionalize (Leadership/Ethics Developed, Doctrine Incorporated, PME improved, Organizations Capable); and, 4) Integrate Regional Activities (Mission Command Executed, Mil-Mil Relationships strengthened, and Regional Architecture Supported). See Figure 2, Introduction.

Privileges and Immunities. As defined in 2 FAM 232.1-1 (U.S. State Department Foreign Affairs Manual) Diplomatic Agents "Diplomatic agents enjoy the highest degree of privileges and immunities. They enjoy complete personal inviolability. This means that: they should not be arrested or detained; they are owed a special measure of respect and protection; and neither their property nor residences may be entered or searched. Diplomatic agents also enjoy complete immunity from the criminal jurisdiction of the host State and thus cannot be prosecuted absent a waiver no matter how serious the offense. Diplomatic agents, with certain exceptions, also have immunity from civil suit. Finally, they enjoy complete immunity from any requirement to provide evidence as witnesses. They also cannot be required to testify, even when they themselves have been the victim of a crime.

Family members forming part of the household of diplomatic agents (recognized by the Department of State as such) enjoy the same privileges and immunities as do the sponsoring diplomatic agents.

Additionally, 2 FAM 232.1-2 Members of Administrative and Technical Staff. "Members of the administrative and technical staff of a diplomatic mission perform tasks critical to the inner workings of the mission. Accordingly, they enjoy immunities identical to those of diplomatic agents in respect of personal inviolability, immunity from criminal jurisdiction, and immunity from any requirement to provide evidence as witnesses. Their immunity from civil jurisdiction, however, is less extensive than that of diplomatic agents. Members of the administrative and technical staff enjoy immunity from civil jurisdiction only in connection with the performance of their official duties."

Lack of a status of forces agreement was another factor that contributed to important differences in how the OSC-I functioned. As the withdrawal deadline neared, the U.S. sought to revise the existing security agreement to permit a U.S. troop presence beyond 2011 due to continuing concerns about the security environment. Despite concerted efforts to renegotiate the security agreement the government of Iraq indicated that it would not extend the legal protections of that document. This did not meet Defense Department requirements for ensuring the security of its personnel in Iraq.

Senior Advisors' Group (SAG). A section in the OSC-I with a mission of enabling Iraqi senior military and civilian leaders to develop the Iraqi institutional capability for internal and external defense across security ministerial functions in order to foster and facilitate a strategic security partnership between the U.S. and Iraq governments. Key tasks included: gain and maintain situational awareness of the Iraqi Ministry of Defense (MoD); facilitate the building of a long term U.S.-Iraq security relationship; foster partnership with Iraqi Joint Headquarters and Ministry of Defense counterparts; and, facilitate key leader engagements. Though activities like those performed by the SAG supported Security Sector Reform, they were not always referred to in that context.

Size of the OSC-I. Since OSC-I's inception in 2009, the overall security cooperation mission in Iraq remained fairly constant. The National Security Council (NSC) Deputies Committee initially approved 157 billets in late 2009 for the OSC-I to support a specific range of security assistance and security cooperation efforts for Iraq (see Appendix D). In late 2011, the NSC Deputies approved an expanded OSC-I that was requested by United States Forces–Iraq and which eventually increased its size to about 260 billets. Instead of expanding its OSC-I mission scope, those increased personnel mostly provided OSC-I the necessary mission support capability that it required, since the OSC-I had a unique responsibility to conduct security cooperation. This was unlike a conventional SCO established in other countries, and there was no follow-on military force with that staff capability which OSC-I could leverage for accomplishing its activities.

Standard Operating Procedures. DoD standard operating procedures are a set of instructions covering those features of operations which lend themselves to a definite or standardized procedure without loss of effectiveness. The procedure is applicable unless ordered otherwise. (JP 1-02, "Department of Defense Dictionary of Military and Associated Terms," November 8, 2010, as amended through April 15, 2013.) The use of SOPs provides institutional knowledge of procedures, continuity of processes, instructions on the performance of routine or repetitive activity, as well as a quality assurance system and evidence of compliance with prescribed policies and requirements. The use of SOPs also facilitates training of new personnel by providing written processes and procedures that reflect the continuity of operations and experiences gained.

Uncertain Environment. Operational environment in which host government forces, whether opposed to or receptive to operations that a unit intends to conduct, do not have totally effective control of the territory and population in the intended operational area. JP 1-02, November 8, 2010, as amended through April 15, 2013.

Withdrawal From Iraq. In the "Agreement Between the United States of America and the Republic of Iraq On the Withdrawal of United States Forces from Iraq and the Organization of Their Activities during Their Temporary Presence in Iraq," effective January 1, 2009, it states in Article 24, "Withdrawal of the United States Forces from Iraq," that "All the United States Forces shall withdraw from all Iraqi territory no later than December 31, 2011."

Appendix D. Office of Security Cooperation–Iraq Security Assistance and Security Cooperation Functions

Introduction

This Appendix is divided into four sections. The first distinguishes only those DoD administered security assistance programs as a subset of the broader security cooperation activities. The second outlines the legislated functions that security cooperation organizations are authorized to perform. The third section lists and defines the specific security assistance and cooperation functions that the Office of Security Cooperation–Iraq was designed to perform. The final section lists the responsibilities of the Senior Defense Official/Defense Attaché (SDO/DATT), as established in DoD Directive 5105.75.

DoD Administered Security Assistance Programs as a Subset of Security Cooperation

U.S. foreign assistance takes three forms: development assistance, humanitarian assistance, and security assistance. DoD administers select security assistance programs for the DOS. Joint Publication 1-02, "Department of Defense Dictionary of Military and Associated Terms,"[1] describes DoD administered security assistance programs as an elemental sub-set of the broader security cooperation activities:

> **Security Assistance** – Group of programs authorized by the Foreign Assistance Act of 1961, as amended, and the Arms Export Control Act of 1976, as amended, or other related statutes by which the United States provides defense articles, military training, and other defense-related services by grant, loan, credit, or cash sales in furtherance of national policies and objectives. Security assistance is an element of security cooperation funded and authorized by Department of State to be administered by Department of Defense/Defense Security Cooperation Agency. [DoD IG note: Only those security assistance programs administered by DoD are a subset of security cooperation.]

> **Security Cooperation** – All Department of Defense interactions with foreign defense establishments to build defense relationships that promote specific U.S. security interests, develop Allied and friendly military capabilities for self-defense and multinational operations, and provide U.S. forces with peacetime and contingency access to a host nation.

It also defines those DoD elements responsible for managing security assistance and security cooperation functions in a foreign country as:

> **Security Cooperation Organization** – All Department of Defense elements located in a foreign country with assigned responsibilities for carrying out security assistance/cooperation management functions. It includes military assistance advisory

---

[1] Latest edition: November 8, 2010 (As Amended Through 15 April 2013).

groups, military missions and groups, offices of defense and military cooperation, liaison groups, and defense attaché personnel designated to perform security assistance/cooperation functions.

The Defense Security Cooperation Agency outlines security assistance as 12 major programs identified in the DSCA Manual 5105.38-M, "Security Assistance Management Manual (SAMM)." While seven of these Foreign Assistance Act and Arms Export Control Act (AECA)-authorized programs are administered by DoD, specifically by DSCA, they remain under the general control of the Department of State as components of U.S. foreign assistance. The seven programs DoD has responsibility for administering are:

- Foreign Military Sales (FMS)
- Foreign Military Construction Services
- Foreign Military Financing Program
- Leases
- Military Assistance Program (MAP)
- International Military Education and Training (IMET)
- Drawdown

Statutory Security Cooperation Office Functions[2]

Section 515, Foreign Assistance Act of 1961, as amended, provides for the President to assign members of the U.S. Armed Forces to a foreign country. It is the governing legislation on what functions those military personnel are authorized to perform, which include:

1. equipment and services case management;
2. training management;
3. program monitoring;
4. evaluation and planning of the host government's military capabilities and requirements;
5. administrative support;
6. promoting rationalization, standardization, interoperability, and other defense cooperation measures; and
7. liaison functions exclusive of advisory and training assistance.

In performing the first function, equipment and services case management, or FMS case management, the SCO serves as the intermediary between the FMS case manager and the host nation to ensure that each case is prepared and executed in accord with host nation

---

[2] This section and the preceding paragraph are primarily derived from: Security Cooperation Organization (SCO) Responsibilities (February 2013) briefing and briefing notes, Defense Institute of Security Assistance Management, http://www.disam.dsca.mil/RESEARCH/presentations.asp, accessed on July 25, 2013, Slides 9 – 22 & 54.

desires. In this regard, the SCO assists the host nation to delineate its requirements in terms of equipment and services. After that, it serves as the facilitator between the United States and host nation to fill those requirements. Notably, while the SCO is involved in case management, their personnel are not normally case managers.

For the second function, training management, SCO personnel should coordinate all military training conducted or contracted by DoD for the host nation. SCO personnel advise and assist in identifying, forecasting, and programming host nation training requirements; bring in mobile training teams, Security Assistance Teams, etc.; and oversee the conduct of the training. Security assistance personnel do not have authority to actually conduct that training. In fact, Congress specifically limits the advisory and training assistance conducted by military personnel assigned under Section 515 authority to an absolute minimum. It is the sense of the Congress that such advising and training assistance activities shall be provided primarily by other personnel who are not assigned under Section 515 and who are detailed for limited periods to perform specific tasks.

The SCO role in the third function, program monitoring, is a very important one that has several aspects. One of the most important aspects involves working with the host country to advise on the best way to integrate the equipment, services, and training they already possess with equipment they are buying and what they are contemplating buying to best meet that country's defense objectives. In the process, SCO should promote interoperability of all systems to further host nation forces combined operations capabilities with U. S. forces. The SCO also supports U. S. defense industries' marketing efforts.

End-use monitoring (EUM) of U.S. origin equipment is another key program monitoring aspect. In some cases EUM involves monitoring the use of sensitive technology or other selected items, which may require the SCO to conduct periodic inventories and inspections of specific items that the United States has sold, transferred, or leased.

Finally, program monitoring also entails providing advice and information on methods of disposal and/or transfer of the items at the end of the useful life of an item in the host nation's inventory and overseeing U.S. leased equipment.

The fourth major SCO function is to evaluate host country military capabilities. First, in the role as advisor to the senior military and defense personnel in a country, the SCO has an opportunity to advise the host country personnel on developing strategies and priorities. Second, the SCO provides information to U.S. decision makers on host country desires and how they meet the foreign policy objectives in the U.S. national security strategy.

In regards to the fifth function, administrative support, the SCO is authorized to perform a range of administrative support functions. These may include, but are not limited to:

- Budget planning and execution
- Accountability for property

- Maintenance of vehicles
- Personnel actions
- Housing and Quality of Life
- Country clearances and U.S. visitor support
- Managing communication and automation equipment
- Arranging for postal services and military support flights and cargo

The sixth function, Rationalization, Standardization, and Interoperability (RSI), is another major SCO function serving U.S. interests. RSI is not limited to standardization of equipment and interchangeability of repair parts. Instead, it covers the full spectrum of operations and logistics, to include military terminology, doctrine, communications, and medical, among other aspects. Basically, if the host nation is obtaining articles, services, and training from the U.S., RSI is being promoted.

SCOs play a key role in implementing U.S. RSI policy. This policy indicates interoperability with partner nations is in the best interests of the United States, but recognizes the degree of international RSI that is subject to financial, legal, technical, and policy considerations.

Finally, to perform the functions just discussed the SCO serves a seventh liaison function. Though Section 515 strictly limits advisory and training assistance activities by military personnel assigned under that section to an absolute minimum, the SCO may perform other duties assigned by the combatant command or the ambassador. For instance, the SCO can play a very important role when the United States is requested or directed to assist in disaster relief in a country. Some members of the SCO may also be tasked for search and rescue duties.

These SCO mandated functions are performed by working with the senior military and civilian defense personnel in the host country. While discouraging SCO personnel from providing operational advice or training, it does allow this to be done by special teams. Overall, the SCO impacts U.S. national security objectives by:

- providing a basis for U.S. access,
- influencing host nation decision-makers,
- strengthening host nation self-defense,
- improving interoperability with U.S. forces,
- strengthening host nation leadership and professional skills, and
- furthering U.S. economic interests.

With this legislative basis, OSC-I was designed to perform specific security assistance and security cooperation functions, which are listed in Table 1 and defined in the next two sections.

Table 1. OSC-I Designed Security Assistance and Cooperation Activities

	OSC Activities	OPR	Action
1	Acquisition and Cross Servicing Agreements	DoD	OSC
2	Acquisition and Cross Servicing Agreements (Significant Military Equipment)	DoD	OSC
3	Aviation Leadership Program	DoD	OSC
4	Building Partner Capacity of Foreign Militaries	DoD	OSC
5	Dept of Defense Regional Centers for Security Studies	DoD	OSC
6	Developing Country Attendance at Bilateral & Multilateral Meetings	DoD	OSC
7	Developing Country Combined Exercise Program	DoD	OSC
8	Direct Commercial Sales	DSCA	OSC
9	Drawdowns	DoD	OSC
10	Embedded and Mobile Training	DoD/DOS	OSC
11	End Use Monitoring	DSCA	OSC
12	Excess Defense Articles	DSCA	OSC
13	Exercise-Related Construction	DoD	OSC
14	Foreign Military Construction Services	DSCA	
15	Foreign Military Financing Program	DSCA	OSC
16	Foreign Military Sales	DSCA	OSC
17	Intelligence Capacity Building	DoD/DOS	ODA*
18	Intelligence Sharing	DoD/DOS	ODA*
19	International Military Education and Training	DSCA	OSC
20	Leases	DSCA	
21	Joint Combined Exercise Training	DoD	OSC
22	Medical Team Deployments	DoD	OSC
23	Military Academies	DoD	OSC
24	Military and Professional Exchange Program	DoD	OSC
25	Multi-lateral Interoperability Program	DoD	OSC
26	Multi-lateral Planners Conference	DoD	OSC
27	Security Force Assistance Activities	DoD	OSC
28	Senior War College	DoD	OSC
29	Special Operations Support to Combat Terrorism	DoD	OSC
30	Third Country Transfers	DSCA	OSC
31	Training and Doctrine Conferences and Working Groups	DoD	OSC

Source: DoD OIG SPO (based on May 19, 2010 Multi-National Force Information Paper)

*OSC-I defers to the Office of the Defense Attaché in matters regarding intelligence sharing, intelligence capacity building, intelligence exercises, joint/combined operations and other intelligence activities that may be conducted by other agencies, services or departments. However, due to the sensitivity of the relationship between the GoI and the U.S. Government, collaboration and coordination between the Office of the Defense Attaché (ODA) and OSC-I is maintained at the most robust level. [Note: These particular Intelligence Capacity Building and Intelligence Sharing activities are discussed in other publications and documents and are not defined within this Appendix.]

OSC-I Design Security Assistance Functions[3]

Of the activities listed above, there are primary security assistance programs that are required to be conducted post-2011, as ongoing FMS cases will carry on through the termination of the current security agreement. These will require continuing support for administration, management, training, fielding, and other related security assistance tasks. In addition, the United States Forces–Iraq (USF-I) Operations Order 11-01, Annex V, Appendix 4 indicates that the OSC-I was to have assumed responsibility for performing all security assistance related functions by its initial operating capability (IOC) date of June 1, 2011. The following lists these primary security assistance programs.

Foreign Military Sales

Foreign Military Sales is a non-appropriated program administered by DSCA through which eligible foreign governments purchase defense articles, services, and training from the U.S. Government. The purchasing government normally pays all costs associated with a sale. There is a signed government-to-government agreement, normally documented on a Letter of Offer and Acceptance (LOA) between the USG and a foreign government. Each LOA is commonly referred to as a "case" and is assigned a unique case identifier for accounting purposes.

Under FMS; military articles, services, and training; may be provided from DoD stocks (Section 21, AECA) or from new procurement (Section 22, AECA). If the source of supply is new procurement, on the basis of having an LOA which has been accepted by the foreign government, the USG agency or Military Department (MILDEP) assigned cognizance for this case is authorized to enter into a subsequent contractual arrangement with U.S. industry in order to provide the article or service requested.

Foreign Military Construction Services

Foreign military construction services is a non-appropriated program administered by DSCA and authorized by Section 29, AECA, to include the sale of design and construction services by the USG to eligible purchasers. The construction sales agreement and sales procedures generally parallel those of FMS and are usually implemented by the MILDEP civil engineering agencies.

Foreign Military Financing Program

The Foreign Military Financing Program (FMFP) is an appropriated program administered by DSCA that has undergone a variety of substantive and terminological changes over the years. At present, the program consists of congressionally appropriated grants and loans which enable eligible foreign governments to purchase U.S. defense articles, services, and training through either FMS or direct commercial sales (DCS). Foreign military sales credit is authorized under the provisions of Sections 23 and 24,

---

[3] Security Assistance program definitions derived from: "The Management of Security Cooperation, Defense Institute of Security Assistance Management," (Greenbook) 32nd Edition, January 2013, pp. 1-1 – 1-7.

AECA, and originally served to provide credit (loans) as an effective means for easing the transition of foreign governments from grant aid, for example, Military Assistance Program and International Military Education and Training, to cash purchases.

Prior to FY 1989, this financing program was variously identified as the Foreign Military Sales Credit Program or the Foreign Military Sales Financing Program. In the FY 1989 "Foreign Operations Appropriations Act" (FOAA), Congress introduced a new title, the FMFP, and the forgiven loan/forgiven credit component of the program was identified as FMFP grants to distinguish them from repayable direct FMFP loans. Also, the terms non-repayable loans or non-repayable credits are often used by various security assistance organizations (including DSCA) in place of the term "FMFP grants."

In FY 1990, the Military Assistance Program was formally merged with the FMFP as Congress adopted an administration proposal for integrating all MAP grant funding into the appropriations account for the FMFP. This appropriated program was administered by DSCA. No MAP funds have been appropriated for subsequent fiscal years, and there is no interest in seeking any such funds for the future. This legislative change, therefore, had the dual effect of causing existing MAP-funded programs to lose their former identity and become FMFP-funded programs and establishing the FMFP as the major U.S. financing program for the acquisition of U.S. defense articles and services by foreign governments.

MAP continues to be identified as a current security assistance program because the MAP provided articles remain throughout the world with the continued requirements for EUM, return to the USG when no longer needed, and any proceeds from a sale to a third country or scrapping being returned to the USG.

Beginning in FY 1992, the "Federal Credit Reform Act of 1992" (P.L. 101-508) changed the method of accounting and budgeting for all government loans, including FMFP loans issued under the AECA. This legislation provides a more accurate portrayal of the true cost of loans by providing new budget authority only for the subsidy element of the loan program and is the basis for the establishment of two new financial accounts:

- The first contains only the FMFP grant portion of the program administrative costs.
- The second account provides the budget authority needed to fund the subsidy element of the proposed loan programs.

While there are previously authorized FMFP loans still being repaid to the USG, this loan element is seldom used; the FMFP grant element (no repayment) is the norm.

Leases

Chapter 6, of the AECA, authorizes the President to lease defense articles to friendly governments or international organizations for up to 5 years (renewable). This non-appropriated program is administered by DSCA. The law allows the lease of defense articles only for compelling foreign policy or national security reasons, and stipulates that the full cost of the lease, with some exceptions, must be borne by the recipient. Furthermore, leased articles must not be needed for U.S. public use during the lease period, and the United States retains the right to terminate the lease at any time.

For the recipient country, leases may be cheaper than purchasing the article outright, and they provide a convenient vehicle for obtaining defense articles for temporary use. Leases are executed through a lease agreement, with an associated FMS case to cover repair, training, supply support, and/or transportation, if required.

International Military Education and Training

The International Military Education and Training program provides grant financial assistance for training in the United States and, in some cases, in overseas facilities to selected foreign military and civilian personnel. In earlier years, grant aid training of foreign military personnel was funded as part of the MAP appropriation. Starting with FY 1976, a separate authorization for IMET was established in Section 541, FAA. This appropriated program is administered by DSCA. Although historically a relatively modest program in terms of cost, both the President and Congress attach significant importance to this program. The recipient countries, likewise, are heavily reliant on this grant program and, in many cases, this program serves as the only method to receive training from the U.S. military.

At a time of declining defense and foreign aid budgets, IMET advances U.S. objectives on a global scale at a relatively small cost. In many countries, having a core group of well-trained, professional leaders with firsthand knowledge of America will make a difference in winning access and influence for our diplomatic and military representatives. Thus, a relatively small amount of IMET funding will provide a return for U.S. policy goals, over the years, far greater than the original investment.

In 1980, Section 644(m)(5), FAA, was amended to authorize IMET tuition costing in terms of the additional costs that are incurred by the USG in furnishing such assistance. Section 21(a)(1)(C), AECA, was also amended to allow IMET recipients to purchase FMS training on an additional cost basis. The practical effects of these changes were to substantially reduce tuition costs for IMET funded students, and thereby increase the amount of training an eligible country can obtain with its IMET grant funds and through FMS purchases.

A new IMET initiative was introduced in the FY 1991 FOAA when Congress adopted a Senate proposed IMET earmark of $1 million to be used exclusively for expanding courses for foreign officers as well as for civilian managers and administrators of defense establishments. The focus of such training is on developing professional level management skills, with emphasis on military justice systems, codes of conduct, and the protection of human rights. Section 541, FAA, was amended to permit non-Ministry of Defense civilian government personnel to be eligible for this program, if such military education and training would:

- Contribute to responsible defense resource management.

- Foster greater respect for and understanding of the principle of civilian control of the military.
- Contribute to cooperation between military and law enforcement personnel with respect to counternarcotics law enforcement efforts.
- Improve military justice systems and procedures in accordance with internationally recognized human rights.

This expanded IMET (E-IMET) program was further extended in FY 1993 to also include participation by national legislators who are responsible for oversight and management of the military. The E-IMET program authority was again amended in 1996 by P.L.104-164 to also include nongovernmental organization personnel.

Drawdowns

During a crisis, Section 506, FAA, authorizes the President to provide USG articles, services, and training to friendly countries and international organizations at no cost, to include free transportation. There is a $100 million ceiling per fiscal year on articles, services, and training provided for military purposes and another fiscal year ceiling of $200 million for articles, services and training required for non-military purposes such as disaster relief, nonproliferation, antiterrorism, counternarcotics, refugee assistance, and Vietnam War-era missing in action/prisoners of war location and repatriation. When emergency support for peacekeeping operations is required, Section 552(c)(2), FAA, separately authorizes the President to drawdown up to $25 million per fiscal year in USG articles and services from any agency. Special drawdown authorities are periodically legislated to include $30 million in support for the Yugoslav International Criminal Court. These non-appropriated authorities are administered by DSCA when defense articles, services, or training from DoD are to be drawn down.

Direct Commercial Sales

DCS are commercial exports of defense articles, services, and training licensed under the authority of Section 38, AECA, made by U.S. defense industry directly to a foreign government. Unlike the procedures employed for FMS, DCS transactions are not administered by DoD and do not normally include a government-to-government agreement. Rather, the required USG controls are implemented through licensing by the Directorate of Defense Trade Controls in the DOS. The day-to-day rules and procedures for these types of sales are contained in the "International Traffic in Arms Regulations" [22 CFR 120-130].

Of note, not all license approvals will result in signed contracts and actual deliveries. Like FMS, DCS deliveries are likely to take place years after the commercial contract is signed and the export license is obtained by U.S. industry.

Other Security Assistance Related Programs

While these following programs are not identified by DSCA in the SAMM as one of the specific security assistance programs, they are very much related to the duties of the security assistance community, both in the United States and recipient foreign governments.

Excess Defense Articles

Excess defense articles identified by the MILDEP or DoD agency are authorized for sale using the FMS authority in Section 21, AECA, and FMS processes identified within the SAMM for property belonging to the USG. Prices range from 5 to 50 percent of original acquisition value, depending on the condition of the article. Additionally, Section 516, FAA, authorizes the President to transfer excess defense articles on a grant basis to eligible countries (justified in the annual Congressional Budget Justification). While excess defense articles can be transferred at no-cost, the recipient must typically pay for any transportation or repair charges. Under certain circumstances, transportation charges may be waived, with the cost absorbed by DoD appropriated funds.

Third-Country Transfers

Section 3(d), AECA, authorizes the President to manage and approve the transfer of U.S.-origin defense articles from the original recipient country to a third country. Requests for third-country transfers are normally approved if the USG is willing to conduct a direct transfer to the third country. Third-country transfer authority to countries must be obtained in writing from the DOS in advance of the proposed transfer. This applies to all U.S.-origin defense articles regardless of the method of original transfer from the USG or U.S. industry.

End-Use Monitoring

This program is a key monitoring responsibility for equipment of U.S. origin. In some cases EUM involves monitoring the use of sensitive technology or other selected items, which may require the SCO to conduct periodic inventories and inspections of specific items that the United States has sold, transferred, or leased.

OSC-I Design Security Cooperation Functions[4]

Besides the core security assistance programs that DoD administers for DOS, other security cooperation activities were also identified that most likely would be required post-2011 to support a foundation of building a defense relationship, developing military capability, and providing access with the partner nation. Descriptions of activities that fall within the scope of OSC-I for management, coordination, or execution and most likely will be enduring are listed in Table 1. In addition to the security assistance functions discussed in the last section that the OSC-I was to assume by its IOC date of June 1, 2011, the OSC-I was supposed to have the capacity of performing these remaining security cooperation functions by its full operating capability (FOC) date of October 1, 2011. Though not delineated in any one source, the following categorizes DoD-authorized security cooperation programs the OSC-I was designed to perform at FOC, with a brief description and references for each program. It should be reiterated

---

[4] Security Assistance program definitions derived from: "The Management of Security Cooperation, Defense Institute of Security Assistance Management," (Greenbook) 32nd Edition, January 2013, pp. 1-7 – 1-26, except for those items annotated with an asterisk (*) in the title. [Note: Items annotated with an asterisk (*) in the title were derived from a USF-I Information Paper, USF-I Enduring Activities, dated January 24, 2010.]

that the previously described FAA and AECA-authorized security assistance programs administered by DoD in accordance with the SAMM also fall under the broad definition of security cooperation.

Acquisition and Cross-Servicing Agreements

Acquisition and cross-servicing agreements (ACSA) are initiated and negotiated by a Geographic Combatant Commander to allow U.S. logistics support of a military unit of another country. Lethal significant military equipment or support reasonably available from U.S. commercial sources may not be provided under an ACSA. The Joint Chiefs of Staff, the Office of the Secretary of Defense, and the Department of State, to include a 30-day advance notification to Congress, must approve the proposal before the agreement is negotiated and concluded by the GCC.

The authority for an ACSA is 10 U.S.C., 2341-2350, with procedures provided in DOD Directive 2010.9. However, the National Defense Authorization Act (NDAA) for FY 2007, P.L.110-417, 109-364, 17 October 2006, Section 1202, as amended, authorized the loan of certain categories of significant military equipment defense articles to countries participating in coalition operations in Iraq, Afghanistan, or for peacekeeping operations for up to 1 year. The authorization is extended through FY 2014. It must be determined by the Secretaries of State and Defense that it is in the U.S. national security interest to provide this loan and there are no unfilled U.S. in-theater requirements for the loaned articles.

Aviation Leadership Program

Section 544(c), FAA, authorizes the cooperative participation of foreign and U.S. military and defense civilian personnel in post-undergraduate flight training and tactical leadership programs at locations in Southwest Asia without charge to participating foreign countries. Such training must satisfy common requirements with the United States for post-undergraduate flight and tactical leadership training. Cooperative arrangements require an equitable contribution of support and services from each participating country. The President may waive the requirement for an equitable contribution of a participating foreign country if he determines that to do so is important to the national security interests of the United States. Costs incurred by the United States shall be charged to the current applicable appropriations accounts or funds of the participating United States Government agencies.

10 U.S.C. 9381-9383 authorizes the Secretary of the Air Force (SAF) to provide undergraduate pilot training and any necessary related training to include language training to students from friendly, less-developed countries. Though aviation leadership program (ALP) students are to be managed and priced as if in the IMET program, IMET funds are not to be used. Any training costs to include actual cost of the training and subsistence are to be incurred by the USAF. DoDI 2010.12 provides guidance to SAF, DSCA, and the CoCOMs for ALP eligibility and implementation.

Building Partner Capacity of Foreign Militaries

Beginning in FY 2006, up to $350 million in DoD funding may be used annually to equip, supply, and train foreign military forces (including maritime security forces) to conduct counterterrorism operations, or participate in or support military and stability operations in which U.S. forces are participating. Any country prohibited by law from receiving such assistance may not receive such assistance. This program is initially authorized by NDAA FY 2006, Section 1206, as amended. This annual "1206" authority for individual programs is to be notified to Congress 15 days prior to implementation, with the funds to be obligated prior to the end of the subject fiscal year. This short time requirement places significant pressure on the MILDEP acquisition agencies for execution. Pseudo LOA case procedures are used for the implementation and management of this program. This program is managed by DSCA and the MILDEPs in support of Assistance Secretary of Defense for Special Operations/Low-Intensity Conflict and the GCC; requests are often initiated by the SCO. Both the Secretaries of Defense and State must concur with proposed programs prior to notifying Congress. Legislative proposals have regularly sought to raise the 1206 cap, and the program is currently authorized through FY 2013.

Department of Defense Regional Centers for Security Studies

Title 10 authorities and DoD appropriations funded the development of five regional centers for security studies. The centers serve as a mechanism for communicating U.S. foreign and defense policies to international students, a means for countries to provide feedback to the United States concerning these policies and communicating country policies to the United States. The regional centers' activities include education, research, and outreach. They conduct multi-lateral courses in residence, seminars within their region, and conferences that address global and regional security challenges, such as terrorism and proliferation. Participants are drawn from the civilian and military leadership of Allied and partner nations. Security assistance funding is not used to pay for the centers or the students attending them.

However, under certain circumstances, DoD funds may be used to fund foreign attendance at the centers. The Under Secretary of Defense for Policy in coordination with the relevant GCC provides oversight for the five centers. DODD 5200.41 provides policy and management guidance. Beginning in FY 2006, DSCA began administering the DoD centers under the direction of the Under Secretary of Defense for Policy. The five centers are:

- Africa Center for Strategic Studies, located at the National Defense University in Fort McNair, Washington, D.C. was established in 1999.
- Asia-Pacific Center for Security Studies, located in Honolulu, Hawaii, was established in 1995.
- Center for Hemispheric Defense Studies, located at the National Defense University in Fort McNair, Washington, D.C., was established in 1997.
- George C. Marshall European Center for Security Studies, located in Garmisch, Germany, was established in 1993.

- Near-East South Asia Center for Strategic Studies, located at the National Defense University in Fort McNair, Washington, D.C., was established in 2000.

Section 904 of the NDAA for FY 2007 finally codified the authority for these regional centers with a new 10 U.S.C., 184.

Payment of Expenses to Attend Bilateral or Regional Conferences

10 U.S.C., 1051 authorizes DoD to pay travel and personal expenses for developing country personnel to attend bilateral or regional conferences, usually GCC sponsored.

Developing Country Combined Exercise Program

The Developing Country Combined Exercise Program (DCCEP) is authorized by 10 U.S.C. 2010 to use DoD funds to pay for incremental expenses for a developing country to participate in a combined exercise with U.S. forces. Such expenses normally include rations, fuel, training ammunition, and transportation. The Joint Staff in coordination with the GCC manages DCCEP. This authority was further amended in FY 2009 with a new 10 U.S.C. 2010(d) authorizing funding for exercise expenses that begin in one fiscal year and extend into the following fiscal year.

Mobile Training Teams and Mobile Education Teams*

This program consists of U.S. military and civilian personnel assigned temporarily in country to train/educate (Mobile Training Teams [MTT] or Mobile Education Teams [MET], respectively) international personnel. MTTs and METs are authorized for specific in-country training requirements, training associated with equipment transfer, or to conduct surveys and assessments of training requirements.

When the request message is received from the SCO and approved for programming, the GCC and military service will verify that it has the capability to provide the training requested and "call up" the team. Once in-country, the team reports to and comes under supervision of the SCO chief.

Exercise Related Construction

The exercise related construction program is authorized by 10 U.S.C. 2805 with policy guidance provided within "Chairman of the Joint Chiefs of Staff Instruction" 4600.01A to allow overseas construction by the U.S. military in locations where there is no permanent U.S. presence. The construction is to enhance exercise effectiveness, enhance troop quality of life, and increase operational readiness. The construction is typically used by U.S. forces during an exercise but remains intact for host nation use after departure. Projects may include new construction, conversion of existing facilities (for example, warehouses into exercise operations centers), and restoration of deteriorating facilities.

The United States and/or the host nation engineer units and construction contracts may be used to accomplish projects. When construction is accomplished with partner nation engineers, interoperability benefits are also obtained. The Joint Staff logistics engineering division manages the program through the engineer divisions of the area GCCs.

Joint Combined Exchange Training

The Joint Combined Exchange Training Program (JCET) includes the deployment by U.S. Special Operations Forces with the dual purpose of training themselves and foreign counterparts. Title 10 United States Code (2011),provides the authority for the use of DoD funding for JCET. This funding can be used for the training of the foreign counterpart, expenses for the U.S. deployment, and, for developing countries, the incremental expenses incurred by the country for the training. The JCET program is carefully followed by Congress because of concerns about inadequate civilian oversight and fears that such training might benefit units or individuals who have committed human rights violations.

In addition to JCET, the NDAA, FY 2005, Section 1208, P.L. 108-375, 28 October 2004, as amended, originally authorized the Secretary of Defense to expend up to $25 million in DoD funding annually to support foreign forces, irregular forces, groups, or individuals engaged in supporting or facilitating ongoing operations by U.S. special operations forces in combating terrorism. This authority is not to be delegated below the Secretary of Defense.

Assignment of DoD Civilian Employees as Advisors to Ministries of Defense*

Section 1081, P.L. 112-81, 31 December 2011, NDAA, FY 2012, authorizes the Secretary of Defense, with the concurrence of the Secretary of State, to assign DoD civilian employees as advisors to ministries of defense (or security agencies serving in a similar defense function) of other countries with the authority to expire at the end of FY 2014. Any assignment of such personnel after FY 2014 may continue but only with the use of funds available for FYs 2012-2014. The functions of such advisors are to include:

- provide institutional, ministerial-level advice, and other training to personnel of the ministry to which assigned to support of stabilization or post-conflict activities; or
- assist such ministry in building core institutional capacity, competencies, and capabilities to manage defense-related processes.

Military Academies and Senior Military Colleges

Military Academy Student Exchanges

By international agreement, the MILDEP secretaries each may authorize up to one hundred students annually to participate in the reciprocal exchange of cadets to attend the appropriate military academies. The authorities for this exchange program are:

- 10 U.S.C. 4345 for the U.S. Military Academy

- 10 U.S.C. 6957a for the U.S. Navy Academy
- 10 U.S.C. 9345 for the U.S. Air Force Academy

Senior Military Colleges and Military Academies

10 U.S.C. 2111b authorizes DoD and the MILDEPs to provide quotas to international students to attend the various senior officer colleges. The MILDEP secretaries each may provide up to 60 quotas at any 1 time to foreign military students to attend the 3 military academies. The Office of the Under Secretary of Defense for Policy may waive all or any part of the requirement to reimburse any cost for attendance. The invitations to apply to attend the academies are offered by the MILDEP secretaries usually through the Office of Defense Attaché. These programs are not considered security assistance; authorities for attending the military academies are:

- 10 U.S.C. 4344(a)(1) for the U.S. Military Academy,
- 10 U.S.C. 6957(a)(1) for the U.S. Navy Academy, and
- 10 U.S.C. 9344(a)(1) for the U.S. Air Force Academy.

Military and Professional Exchange Program

Professional Military Education Student Exchanges

Section 544(a), FAA, authorizes by international agreement no-cost, reciprocal professional military education (PME) student exchanges. PME usually includes attendance at the MILDEP leadership and management education institutions but not to include the service academies. The U.S. participant in this program will attend the equivalent institution in the foreign country and be administratively supported by either the local Office of Defense Attaché or SCO.

Defense Personnel Exchange Program

The NDAA for FY 1997, Section 1082, authorizes DoD to enter into reciprocal personnel exchange agreements with a country for personnel to be assigned to each other's organizations. Though not codified into 10 U.S.C., this authority has no expiration date. Each country is to pay any associated costs with the exchange. Exceptions to this requirement are temporary duty costs and training directed by the host country.

Multilateral Military Centers of Excellence

Section 1232, P.L. 110-417, 14 October 2008, NDAA, FY 2009, provided for a new 10 U.S.C., authorizing DoD, in coordination with DOS, to participate by memorandum of understanding in any multilateral military center of excellence for the following purposes:

- Enhancing other countries' military and civilian personnel to engage in joint exercises or coalition of international military operations.
- Improve interoperability between U.S. forces and other countries' forces.

DoD Operations and Maintenance funds may be used to pay the U.S. share of operating any such center and to pay expenses to attend such centers.

Center for Complex Operations

Section 1031, P.L. 110-417, 14 October 2008, NDAA, FY 2009, provided for a new 10 U.S.C. authorizing the establishment of a center for complex operations. The purpose of the center is:

- Effective coordination in the preparation of DoD and other USG personnel for complex operations.
- Foster unity of effort among USG organizations, foreign government personnel international non-governmental organizations (NGOs), and U.S. NGOs during complex operations.
- Conduct research, collect, analyze, and distribute lessons learned and compile best practices.
- Identify gaps in the education and training of USG personnel and facilitate efforts to fill any such gaps.

Prior concurrence from DOS is required before including other countries or international NGOs. Complex operations include stability operations, security operations, transition and reconstruction operations, counterinsurgency operations, and irregular warfare. The Center for Complex Operations (CCO) has been established and located at the National Defense University (NDU) on Fort Leslie McNair in Washington, D.C., since early 2009.

Security Force Assistance

Security Force Assistance is DoD activities that contribute to the unified action by the USG to support the development of the capacity and capability of foreign security forces and their supporting institutions. SFA is a subset of DoD security cooperation and security assistance provides critical tools to fund and enable SFA activities. Activities are carried out by the civilian expeditionary workforce alongside general purpose forces and special operations forces.

Other Military-to-Military Contact and Security Cooperation Programs

Though not specifically listed in the proposed OSC-I design functions, the following lists a number of other security cooperation related programs that it might be involved in supporting. Many of these programs have been around for a long time and continue today as a general program to establish and strengthen professional (and personal) relationships between two country counterparts.

Traditional Combatant Commander Activities

Section 168, title 10, United States Code, authorizes DoD, normally the GCC, to conduct military-to-military contacts and comparable activities with allied and friendly countries to encourage a democratic orientation of defense establishments and military forces. Some functions include:

- Seminars and conferences
- Exchange of military and civilian personnel
- DoD personnel expenses
- Military liaison teams
- Distribution of publications

Funding for the Traditional Combatant Commander Activities program is provided to the GCC by the MILDEPs will act as executive agents. Section 1202, P.L. 110-417, provided a new 10 U.S.C. 168(e)(5) authorizing the use of funds for such expenses that begin in one fiscal year and extended into the following fiscal year.

Combatant Commander Initiative Fund

The Combatant Commander Initiative Fund consists of GCC-nominated special interest programs authorized by 10 U.S.C. 166a to be funded at a rate of $25 million annually. The FY 2012 DoD appropriations act provided $47 million for Combatant Commander Initiative Fund (see also Appendix D).

Regional Defense Combating Terrorism Fellowship Program

The Regional Combating Terrorism Fellowship Program (CTFP) was established in 2002 first with DoD funding, later with DoD authorizations, and now under 10 U.S.C. 2249c. The purpose of the program is to help key partner nations cooperate with the United States in the fight against international terrorism by providing education and training on a grant basis to foreign military and civilian personnel. The objective is to bolster the capacity of friends and allies to detect, monitor, interdict, and disrupt the activities of terrorist networks, ranging from weapons trafficking and terrorist-related financing to actual operational planning by terrorist groups. The Assistant Secretary of Defense for Special Operations/Low Intensity Conflict is the Office of the Secretary of Defense Manager of CTFP, in coordination with the GCCs. The day-to-day administration of the program is performed by DSCA. The $20 million was originally appropriated to DoD for CTFP. The management of quotas is very similar to that of IMET. Section 1204, P.L.109-364, amended the annual funding authority to $25 million. Later, Section 1214 of P.L. 110-417 amended the authorized annual funding level to $35 million.

Senior Defense Official/Defense Attaché Responsibilities

DoD Directive 5105.75 establishes the SDO/DATT responsibilities and stipulates that the SDO/DATT in each embassy shall:

- Serve as Defense Attaché and Chief of Security Assistance under the joint oversight and administrative management of the USD(P) and USD(I) through the Directors, DSCA and DIA, in coordination with the GCC.
- Act as the in-country focal point for planning, coordinating, supporting, and/or executing U.S. defense issues and activities in the host nation, including Theater Security Cooperation programs under the oversight of the GCC.

- Serve as the principal embassy liaison with host-nation defense establishments and actively participate in national security and operational policy development and coordination.
- Represent the Secretary of Defense and the DoD Components to host-nation counterparts and foreign diplomats accredited to the host nation, and act as the principal in-country DoD diplomatic representative of the Secretary of Defense and the DoD Components.
- Present coordinated DoD views on all defense matters to the COM and act as the single DoD point of contact to the COM to assist in carrying out the COM's responsibilities under appropriate references.
- Represent the Secretary of Defense and appropriate Commanders of the Combatant Commands for coordination of administrative and security matters for all DoD personnel not under the command of a U.S. area military commander.
- Carry out the duties and instructions as set forth in Chairman Joint Chiefs of Staff Instruction C-3310.01C.
- Exercise Coordinating Authority over DoD elements under the direction and supervision of the COM. This shall not preempt the authority exercised over these elements by the COM, the mission authority exercised by the parent DoD components, or the command authority exercised by the GCC under the Unified Command Plan. Additionally, this authority does not include authority to impose punishment under the Uniform Code of Military Justice.
- As required, provide information to U.S. Government officials on the general scope of in-country activities for all DoD component command elements assigned to the mission. This includes the missions, locations, organization, and unique security requirements.[5]

---

[5] DoD Directive 5105.75, "Department of Defense Operations at U.S. Embassies," December 21, 2007, pp.7-8.

Appendix E. Organizations Contacted and Visited

We visited, contacted, or conducted interviews with officials (or former officials) from the following U.S. and Iraqi organizations:

Government of the United States

U.S. Congress

Senate

- Committee on Armed Services (Professional Staff Members)

House of Representatives

- Committee on Armed Services (Professional Staff Members)

Department of State

Washington, D.C.

- Bureau of Near East Affairs
- Office of Inspector General

U.S. Embassy - Baghdad

- Baghdad Diplomatic Support Center
- Chief of Mission
- Deputy Chief of Mission
- Management Section
- Political Military Section
- Regional Security Officer Section

Department of Defense

Office of the Secretary of Defense (OSD)

- Office of the Under Secretary of Defense for Policy–Principal Director for Middle East Policy
- Office of the Under Secretary of Defense (Comptroller)

Joint Staff

- Director, Strategic Plans and Policy (J5)
- Director, Joint Force Development (J7)

U.S. Central Command

- Headquarters

- o CCJ1–Manpower
- o CCJ3–Operations Directorate
- o CCJ4–Logistics Directorate
- o CCJ5–Strategy, Plans and Policy Directorate
- o CCJ7–Training and Exercises Directorate
- o CCJ8–Resources and Analysis Directorate
- o CCJA–Judge Advocate

- Office of Security Cooperation–Iraq
  - o J1 (Personnel)
  - o J2 (Intel)
  - o J3 (Operations)
  - o J4 (Logistics)
  - o J5 (Plans)
  - o J6 (Command, Control, Communications and Computers)
  - o J7 (Engineering)
  - o J8 (Finance)
  - o J9 (Strategic Communications)
  - o OSC-I Chaplain
  - o OSC-I Chief of Staff
  - o OSC-I Counter Terrorism Service
  - o OSC-I Command Sergeant Major
  - o OSC-I Chief's Initiative Group
  - o OSC-I Deputy
  - o OSC-I Executive Director for Support
  - o OSC-I Explosive Ordnance Disposal Exploitation Chief
  - o OSC-I Inspector General
  - o OSC-I Knowledge Management Officer
  - o OSC-I Professional Military Education
  - o OSC-I Security Assistance Section
    - Security Assistance Air Defense Artillery Team Chief
    - Security Assistance Army Team Chief
    - Security Assistance Air Force Team Chief
    - Security Assistance Army Air Team Chief
    - Security Assistance Log Chief
    - Security Assistance Navy Team Chief
  - o OSC-I Senior Advisor Group
  - o OSC-I Staff Judge Advocate
  - o OSC-I Surgeon

DoD Managed Sites in Iraq Visited

- Besmaya
- Baghdad Diplomatic Support Center–OSC-I
- Embassy Military Attaché and Security Assistance Annex
- Taji

Defense Agencies

- Army and Air Force Exchange Service
- Army Support Command Liaison
- Center for Army Lessons Learned Liaison
- Defense Contract Audit Agency
- Defense Contract Management Agency
- Defense Logistics Agency–Iraq
- Defense Security Cooperation Agency
- Force Protection Division–Iraq
- United States Army Corps of Engineers
- National Capabilities and Resources Office

Government of Iraq

Ministry of Defense

- Chief of Staff, Iraqi Joint Headquarters

This Page Intentionally Left Blank

Appendix F. Management Comments

OFFICE OF THE ASSISTANT SECRETARY OF DEFENSE
WASHINGTON, DC 20301-2400

INTERNATIONAL
SECURITY AFFAIRS

SEP 10 2013

MEMORANDUM FOR DEPUTY INSPECTOR GENERAL, SPECIAL PLANS AND
OPERATIONS

SUBJECT: Response to Draft Report on the Assessment of the Office of Security Cooperation–
Iraq Mission Capability (Project No. D2012-D00SPO-0205.000)

1. The Office of the Under Secretary of Defense for Policy has reviewed the DoD IG Draft
Report (D2012-D00SPO-0205.000) "Assessment of the Office of Security Cooperation–
Iraq Mission Capability." We concur with Recommendations 1.a.(1), 1.a.(2), 1.a.(3), and
4.b.

2. The point of contact for this issue is Lauren Haber at (703)571-2513,
Lauren.Haber2.civ@mail.mil.

Edward M. Minahan
Brig Gen US Air Force
Principal Director (Middle East)

UNITED STATES CENTRAL COMMAND
7115 SOUTH BOUNDARY BOULEVARD
MACDILL AIR FORCE BASE, FLORIDA 33621-5101

01 August 2013

FROM: USCENTCOM Inspector General, Executive Director
TO: JOINT STAFF J7/JDD

SUBJECT: DODIG D2012-DooSPO-0205.000 Draft Report "Office of Security
Cooperation-Iraq Mission Capability" (U)

Ref: (a) JSAP 13-02880

1. (U) In response to Reference (a), the attached consolidated USCENTCOM/OSC-I
response is provided.

2. (U) My POC is ███████████████████████████████████.

DUANE T. RACKLEY
GS15, DAF
Executive Director

Attachment:
TAB A: Consolidated Response (S/REL)

DODIG DRAFT REPORT – DATED 28 June 13
DODIG Project No. D2012-D0SPO-0205.000

Assessment of the Office of Security Cooperation-Iraq Mission Capabilities

CENTCOM and OSC-I COMMENTS
to the DRAFT REPORT

(U) RECOMMENDATION 1.b. (page 18, DODIG Draft Report)
Commander, U.S. Central Command issue an updated Theater Campaign Plan and, in coordination with U.S. Chief of Mission in Iraq, and updated Iraq Country Plan.

(U) CENTCOM RESPONSE: Concur with comment.

(U) Commander, USCENTCOM has issues an updated Theater Campaign Plan Change 3, dated 15 March 2013, which includes a new Intermediate Military Objective (IMO) for Iraq within the Build Partner Capacity Line of Effort (LOE). In addition, USCENTCOM J5 produced an updated Annex O Security Cooperation and Iraq Country Security Cooperation Plan (CSCP) to support the new IMO for Iraq. The Iraq CSCP was developed in coordination with OSC-I and synchronized with the FY 2014 Mission Resource Request (MRR) for Iraq.

(U) The TCP, Annex O, and Iraq CSCP are iterative processed intending to address CENTCOM's objectives in Iraq for the near future. CENTCOM plans to update them annually or as necessary.

(U) RECOMMENDATION 2. (page 24, DODIG Draft Report)
Commander, U.S. Central Command, in coordination with the Under Secretary of Defense for Policy, U.S. Chief of Mission in Iraq, and Chairman of the Joint Chiefs of Staff:

a. (U) Identify and prioritize DoD security cooperation requirements needed to support updated Iraq Country Plan objectives, to include numbers of personnel and skill sets necessary to perform essential activities;
b. (U) Assess the risk to meeting theater and country-specific level planning objectives that result from various models to resource the Office of Security Cooperation-Iraq and other security cooperation requirements in Iraq; and,
c. (U) Advise Chairman of the Joint Chiefs of Staff of risk assessment results in order to inform the required Secretary of Defense reporting on the Office of Security Cooperation – Iraq mandated by the National Defense Authorization Act for Fiscal Year 2013.

(U) CENTCOM RESPONSE: Concur with comment.

(U) If various models to resource OSC-I are defined as different OSC-I personnel manning templates, then we assess moderate risk in meeting theater and country specific level planning objectives with an OSC-I comprised of reduced personnel. As personnel are reduced, there is an expected increase to operational risks in the short term due to reduced key leader engagement opportunities, but also an expected reduction to security related risks due to lessened exposure.

(U) Currently, there is deliberative interagency planning regarding the OSC-I scope and size. OSC-I is scheduled to reduce their personnel strength to 127 by September 30, 2013 and will further reduce to 59 personnel by FY15.

(U) RECOMMENDATION 3.a. (page 31, DODIG Draft Report)
Commander, U.S. Central Command, in coordination with:
- (1) (U) Under Secretary of Defense for Policy and Director of the Joint Staff, evaluate the Office of Security Cooperation – Iraq mission to validate personnel requirements necessary for coordinating and managing security cooperation activities and submit request for Joint Table of Distribution to permanently assign personnel to the Joint Staff.
- (2) (U) Director, Defense Security Cooperation Agency, and Chief, Office of Security Cooperation – Iraq, expedite obtaining the required training for all Office of Security Cooperation – Iraq personnel, as required by Department of Defense Directives and Instructions.
- (3) (U) Chief, Office of Security Cooperation – Iraq, establish a plan for transitioning responsibility for conducting security cooperation activities in Iraq, including the training and advisory activities referred to in the Foreign Assistance Act of 1961, as amended, to U.S. Central Command and other elements for execution.

(U) CENTCOM RESPONSE: Concur with comment.

(U) 3.a.(1): The Joint Staff validated OSC-I JTD requirements in 2010 and the VCJCS endorsed the gain of 46 billets to CENTCOM's JTD for OSC-I. CENTCOM continues to present OSD with manpower requirements for resource decisions through the Program Budget Review. When OSD issues a resource management decision to transition OSC-I to the JTD, CENTCOM will be able to add the billets to the JTD; Services will add to their documents and begin assigning permanent military/civilian personnel.

(U) 3.a.(2): Security Cooperation Management (SCM) training for personnel assigned to Security Cooperation Organizations (SCO) is a high priority for CENTCOM. Services ensure incoming OSC-I personnel have orders reflecting necessary training such as courses offered at the Defense Institute Security Assistance Management (DISAM). Subsequently, CENTCOM J5-SC coordinates with OSC-I, DSCA, and DISAM to maximize the number of personnel that attend DISAM courses before arriving in Baghdad. Personnel who do not receive formal SCM training prior to reporting to OSC-I are required to attend a course offered by a mobile training team or utilize the online training offered by DISAM.

(U) When billets are added to the JTD, each will reflect the training requirements and CENTCOM J1 will state such on requests for fill to the Services in accordance with current directives and policies.

2

(U) This is a recurring requirement.

(U) 3.a.(3): Currently, there is deliberative interagency coordination on better defining the USG long-term strategy and inherent mission requirements. The US Mission-Iraq is on a glide-path to assume a normalized mission similar to other country teams.

(U) The OSC-I personnel will complete transition to the Embassy compound by September 30, 2013 to assume a structure similar to other regional security operation offices.

(U) RECOMMENDATION 3.b. (page 31, DODIG Draft Report)
(U) Chief, Office of Security Cooperation – Iraq, in coordination with U.S. Chief of Mission in Iraq and Commander U.S. Central Command, establish requirements necessary for consolidating the Office of Security Cooperation – Iraq activities within the U.S. Mission Iraq, including development and publishing of Standard Operating Procedures for all critical activities to facilitate full integration in minimum time.

(U) OSC-I RESPONSE: Concur with comment.

(U) OSC-I completed Tikrit site closure and transition to Government of Iraq (GOI) and is on track to complete site transition to Taji, Besmaya by September 30, 2013. OSC-I has transitioned 90% of the Embassy Military Attaché and Security Assistance Annex (EMASSA) office functions to the Baghdad Embassy Compound (BEC) with a September 1, 2013 target to have functions and personnel transitioned to the BEC. Security functions and responsibilities formalized in a security MOA between OSC-I and the U.S. Embassy in Baghdad take effect August 1, 2013.

(U) OSC-I continues to formalize administrative standard operating procedures between OSC-I and the U.S. Embassy in Baghdad.

(U) RECOMMENDATION 4.a. (page 36, DODIG Draft Report)
Commander, U.S. Central Command, in coordination with Chief, Office of Security Cooperation – Iraq, identify the requirements for fully transitioning Department of Defense designated sites in Iraq back to the Government of Iraq, to include adjusting the transition timelines if necessary.

3

(U) RECOMMENDATION 5.a. (page 24, DODIG Draft Report)
Commander, U. S. Central Command, in coordination with Under Secretary of Defense for Policy and Director, Joint Force Development, Joint Staff J7:

    (1) initiate a recommendation for fast track development of doctrine that covers transition of security cooperation and other responsibilities between the Department of Defense and Department of State in the post-contingency environment as has been occurring in Iraq beginning in 2011 and will need to be applied in Afghanistan post- 2014;

    (2) systematically compile and formally submit joint lessons learned to ensure observations and insights emerging from ongoing post-contingency transition activities are captured and incorporated into joint doctrine; and,

    (3) review and recommend changes to appropriate joint doctrine publications to ensure they effectively reflect the doctrinal aspects of planning for and conducting security cooperation and other transition activities in a post-contingency environment.

(U) CENTCOM RESPONSE: Concur with comment.

CENTCOM is willing and, given appropriate lead times, able to contribute as part of the enterprise to developing Joint Doctrine. In this case specifically, Para. 5.a. (1) suggests rushing the development of doctrine to inform currently ongoing planning and preparation for end of contingency operations (OEF) in December 2014. Given a current planning timeline based largely on lessons learned from Operation Iraqi Freedom to produce a transition plan by 1st QTR, FY14 any doctrine developed is already late for informing this planning. Lessons learned from the transition planning during OIF suggest that planning needs to be published for execution one year out. However, an evolving end-state with yet to be determined directed force levels requires an adaptive approach. Adding development of Joint Doctrine for a planning process currently ongoing will be an unacceptable tax on the limited planning resources in the Command.

GENERAL COMMENTS ON THE REPORT

(U) 1. Page 39, paragraph 3.a., line 1. Recommend inserting a change to read: Under Secretary of Defense for Policy and Director of the Joint Staff, evaluate the Office of Security Cooperation – Iraq mission to validate and resource personnel requirements necessary for coordinating and managing security cooperation activities and submit request to the Program Budget Review for Joint Table of Distribution billet authorizations so Services can to permanently assign personnel to OSC-I the Joint Staff.

4

Reply ZIP Code:
20318-7000

2 AUG 13

MEMORANDUM FOR THE OFFICE OF THE DEPUTY INSPECTOR GENERAL FOR
SPECIAL PLANS & OPERATIONS

Subject: Assessment of Office of Security Cooperation-Iraq (OSC-I) Mission
Capabilities

1.   Thank you for the opportunity to comment on the Department of Defense
Office of Inspector General's draft report "*Assessment of OSC-I Mission
Capabilities.*" Transitioning of security cooperation activities from DOD-lead
contingency operations to DOS-lead, Phase 0, steady-state activities is an emerging
and relevant field that is currently being developed in joint doctrine.

2.   This is an interim response pending USCENTCOM's position. The Joint
Staff, in coordination with USD (P)/ DSCA, concurs with comment to the report's
five (5) observations and recommendations. In consultation with the Joint Staff,
the Joint Community, and authors of the report, I clarified the issues and actions
taken which are enclosed for your consideration. Further, the J-7 directed JP 3-
XX, *Military Support to Security Cooperation*, to be published next year, will provide
security cooperation doctrine for planners and facilitate a more productive dialogue
with our partners in the US government.

3.   The Joint Staff/J7 Action Officer is ██████████████████████.

JEROME M. LYNES
Deputy Director, Joint Education and
Doctrine, Joint Staff, J-7

Enclosures:
1- Joint Staff response to DODIG report
2- NDAA Report for FY13
3- U.S. Mission in Iraq Mission Resource Request (MRR)
4- DODD 5105.75, Department of Defense Operations at U.S. Embassies

ENCLOSURE 1

JOINT STAFF COMMENTS to the "Department of Defense Office of Inspector General Report:

- **RECOMMENDATION 1.a.** Under Secretary of Defense for Policy (USD(P)), in coordination with Department of State counterparts and Commander, U.S. Central Command (USCENTCOM):

  (1) clearly specify the nature and scope of OSC-I mission activities, to include security assistance, as well as necessary security cooperation activities;

  (2) take action to ensure interagency information exchange at all DoD echelons is sufficient to effectively plan and execute approved security cooperation activities in Iraq, to include defining a normal OSC-I organizational construct with specific functions; and,

  (3) designate a Senior Defense Official with clearly specified and fully coordinated responsibilities in Iraq.

  J-5 – Concurs with recommendation. J-5 continues to coordinate with USD (P), USCENTCOM and OSC-I to formally designate a Senior Defense Official/Defense Attaché IAW DOD Directive 5105 75, *Department of Defense Operations at U.S. Embassy*, Section 5.9. In the interim, the OSC-I chief will perform these duties until the security cooperation office transitions to a traditional security office.

- **RECOMMENDATION 1.b.** Commander, U. S. Central Command issue an updated Theater Campaign Plan and, in coordination with U.S. Chief of Mission in Iraq, an updated Iraq Country Plan.

  J-5 – Concurs with recommendation. J-5 continues to coordinate with USCENTCOM while they update their Theater Campaign Plan and Country Plan.

- **RECOMMENDATION 2.** Commander, U.S. Central Command, in coordination with USD(P), U.S. Chief of Mission in Iraq, and Chairman of the Joint Chiefs of Staff (CJCS):

  (1) identify and prioritize DOD security cooperation requirements needed to support updated Iraq Country Plan objectives, to include numbers of personnel and skill sets necessary to perform essential activities;

  (2) assess the risk to meeting theater and country-specific level planning objectives that result from various models to resource the Office of Security Cooperation - Iraq and other security cooperation requirements in Iraq; and,

(3) advise Chairman of the Joint Chiefs of Staff of risk assessment results in order to inform the required Secretary of Defense reporting on the OSC-I mandated by the NDAA for Fiscal Year 2013.

J-5 – Concurs with recommendation. Accordingly, J-5 coordinated with USD(P) and USCENTCOM which resulted in the attached Report for FY2013 NDAA and Mission Resource Request – Iraq. The NDAA Report for FY2013 provides the country team guidance regarding security cooperation. COMPLETED on 26 Mar 13/04 Jun 13.

- **RECOMMENDATION 3.a.** Commander, U.S. Central Command, in coordination with:

(1) Under Secretary of Defense for Policy and Director of the Joint Staff, evaluate the OSC-I mission to validate personnel requirements necessary for coordinating and managing security cooperation activities and submit request for Joint Table of Distribution to permanently assign personnel to the Joint Staff.

USD-P (DSCA) – Concurs with recommendation. DSCA, in coordination with USD (P) and USCENTCOM, has conducted a review and validation of personnel requirements to establish and support forty-six (46) security assistance (SA) positions at OSC-I.

J-1 – Concurs with recommendation. J-1 continues to support USCENTCOM's efforts to transition OSC-I to a permanent manning solution supported by a Joint Table of Distribution. JS J-1 POC for OSC-I transition status to a traditional Security Cooperation Organization (SCO) within the US Embassy - Iraq is ███████████, Human Capital Division ███████,J-1, Manpower and Personnel Directorate, Comm: ████████████████ POC for temporary requirement management supporting OSC-I is ████ ██████████ Program Analyst, Personnel Readiness Division Manpower and Personnel Directorate, Comm; ████████████████████.

(2) Director, Defense Security Cooperation Agency (DSCA), and Chief, OSC-I, expedite obtaining the required training for all OSC-I personnel, as required by DOD Directives and Instructions.

USD- P (DSCA) – Concurs with recommendation. Accordingly, DSCA has been coordinating with the Defense Institute for Security Assistance Management (DISAM) Commandant to expedite DISAM training for incoming OSC-I personnel. According to DISAM Course Rosters for the FY-13 Overseas Course sessions to date a total of 56 students were OSC-I bound. DISAM sent a mobile training team (MTT) to OSC-I in March and September, 2012 to conduct training for U.S. personnel only, 102 personnel received training during these events. Although it is unclear how many of these personnel are still assigned to

OSC-I, DISAM is planning to send a MTT to Iraq in September 2013 to conduct additional training sessions for U.S. personnel.

(3) Chief, OSC-I, establish a plan for transitioning responsibility for conducting security cooperation activities in Iraq, including the training and advisory activities referred to in the Foreign Assistance Act of 1961, as amended, to U.S. Central Command and other elements for execution.

J-5 – Concurs with recommendation. Accordingly, J-5 coordinated with USD(P) and USCENTCOM which resulted in the attached Report for FY2013 NDAA and Mission Resource Request – Iraq. The FY2013 NDAA provides guidance and outlines the transition plan for OSC-I integration into the U.S. mission.

- **RECOMMENDATION 3.b.** Chief, OSC-I, in coordination with the U.S. Chief of Mission in Iraq and Commander, U.S. Central Command, establish requirements necessary for consolidating the OSC-I activities within the U.S. Mission Iraq, including development and publishing of Standard Operating Procedures for all critical activities to facilitate full integration in minimum time.

  J-5 – Concurs with recommendation. J-5 coordinated with USCENTCOM which resulted in the attached Report for FY2013 NDAA showing the transition plan for OSC-I integration into the U.S. mission. PROJECTED COMPLETION DATE: 30 Sep 13. J-5 continues to communicate sufficient details about OSC-I capabilities, activities and objectives to U.S. Country Team officials to enable their support, guidance and oversight.

- **RECOMMENDATION 4.a.** Commander, U.S. Central Command, in coordination with Chief, OSC-I, identify the requirements for fully transitioning Department of Defense designated sites in Iraq back to the Government of Iraq, to include adjusting the transition timelines if necessary.

- **RECOMMENDATION 4.b.** USD (P), in coordination with Under Secretary of Defense for Acquisition, Technology, and Logistics (USD-AT&L) and CJCS, take action to ensure necessary resources are available and allocated to U.S. Central Command in order to effectively transfer DOD designated sites in Iraq back to the Government of Iraq.

  J-4 – Concurs with both recommendations. J-4 continues to work with DOD and USCENTCOM to transition DOD sites in Iraq. The transition of DOD sites in Iraq is outlined in the attached Report for FY2013 NDAA. POC is ▮▮▮▮▮▮▮

- **RECOMMENDATION 5.a.** Commander, U. S. Central Command, in coordination with USD (P) and Director, Joint Force Development, Joint Staff J7:

  (1) initiate a recommendation for fast track development of doctrine that covers transition of security cooperation and other responsibilities between the DOD

and DOS in the post-contingency environment as has been occurring in Iraq beginning in 2011 and will need to be applied in Afghanistan post-2014.

(2) systematically compile and formally submit joint lessons learned to ensure observations and insights emerging from ongoing post-contingency transition activities are captured and incorporated into joint doctrine.

(3) review and recommend changes to appropriate joint doctrine publications to ensure they effectively reflect the doctrinal aspects of planning for and conducting security cooperation and other transition activities in a post-contingency environment.

J-7 – Concurs with recommendation. In accordance with CJCS Instruction 5120.02C, Joint Staff, Combatant Commands, Military Services and USD (P) are in the process of reviewing the J-7 directed Preliminary Coordination Program Directive (PCPD) for JP 3-XX, *Military Support to Security Cooperation.*

Accordingly, J-7 continues to work with the National Defense University (NDU) Center for Complex Operations (CCO) and the US Army Center for Lessons Learned (CALL) to incorporate lessons learned into JP 3-XX, *Military Support to Security Cooperation* and other applicable joint publications, specifically JP 3-0, *Joint Operations,* JP 3-07, *Stability Operations,* JP 3-08, *Interorganizational Coordination During Joint Operations,* and JP 5-0, *Joint Operation Planning.* (Reference: CJCSI 3150.25D)

- **RECOMMENDATION 5.b.** Director, Joint Force Development, Joint Staff J7, in accordance with CJCS Instruction 5120.02C and in coordination with USD (P) and Commander, U.S. Central Command, review joint doctrine and provide recommendations for consolidating emerging information from the situation in Iraq as it relates to conducting security cooperation and transitioning responsibilities between DOD and other departments in complex, uncertain post-contingency security environments. (Reference: CJCSI 5120.01C)

J-7 – Concurs with recommendation. In accordance with CJCS Instruction 5120.02C, a thorough review of applicable joint doctrine has been conducted, resulting in the development of JP 3-XX, *Military Support to Security Cooperation.* J-7 will incorporate the National Defense University (NDU) Center for Complex Operations (CCO) *Security Transition Planning Doctrine Proposal,* and the US Army Center for Arms Lessons Learned (CALL), *Senior Leader's Guide to Transition Planning* lessons learned into JP 3-XX, *Military Support to Security Cooperation.* Moreover, lessons learned from security cooperation and transitioning responsibilities will be infused in applicable existing joint doctrine during programed revision cycles.

www.ingramcontent.com/pod-product-compliance
Lightning Source LLC
Chambersburg PA
CBHW080309290526
45790CB00005B/1981